How to Save Your Inner Wonder Woman:

A Guide to Help Caregivers and Allies of
Survivors of Childhood Sexual Abuse Using
Wonder Woman

By Kenneth Rogers, Jr.

Strategic Book Publishing and Rights Co.

Strategic Book Publishing and Rights Co., LLC
USA | Singapore
www.sbpra.net

For information about special discounts for bulk purchases, please contact Strategic Book Publishing and Rights Co., LLC. Special Sales, at bookorder@sbpra.net.

ISBN: 978-1-951530-72-3

Dedication

For Sarah, Susan, Michael, James, and you. Thank you for all you do to help survivors.

BOOKS BY KENNETH ROGERS, JR.

Nonfiction

How to Master Your Inner Superman: A Guide for Male Survivors of Childhood Sexual Abuse Using Superman to Help Conquer the Need for Facades

- Reader's Favorite Book Award Five Star Review

How to Kill Your Batman: A Guide for Male Survivors of Childhood Sexual Abuse Using Batman to Heal Hypervigilance

- NABE Pinnacle Achievement Book Award
- Reader's Favorite Book Award Five Star Review
- Independent Publisher Award: Distinguished Favorite
- National Indie Book Award

Heroes, Villains and Healing: A Guide for Male Survivors of Childhood Sexual Abuse Using DC Superheroes and Villains

- Independent Press Award
- National Indie Book Award
- Beverly Hills Book Award
- NABE Pinnacle Achievement Book Award

Raped Black Male: A Memoir

Young Adult Fantasy

Chronicles of the Last Liturian Book One: The Diary of Oliver Lee

Chronicles of the Last Liturian Book Two: Love and Fear

Chronicles of the Last Liturian Book Three: Infinite Truths and Impossible Dreams

Science Fiction

Sequence

- Next Generation Indie Book Award
- NABE Pinnacle Achievement Book Award

Speculative Fiction

Thoughts in Italics

Writing in the Margins

Table of Contents

Introduction

"Every living thing is beautiful. Unique, and entitled to its own dignity. Love does not dominate. Love does not impose its own will. Does not mistake fear for hate. Love, my child, is our true power, through which we are more than conquerors."

—**Queen Hippolyta**, *Justice League #42*, "Justice Lost: Part 4" (2018)

I must confess, before beginning to research *How to Save Your Inner Wonder Woman*, I was not a fan of the superpowered heroine. I knew of her ability to deflect bullets with her Bracelets of Submission and compel villains to tell the truth using her golden lasso, but there was not much more. I knew she had a connection to the Greek gods and goddesses of old, but how or why escaped my understanding. Why did she need an invisible plane if she could fly? And is *she* bulletproof, or just her bracelets? Even following the release of the 2017 *Wonder Woman* movie (which was awesome), there was no appeal to learn more about the Amazon warrior princess. Researching her timeline throughout the DC universe seemed too time-consuming of a task for a character who used to be the Justice League's personal secretary.

However, as I traveled to conferences across the country, telling my story as a male survivor of childhood sexual abuse and speaking with survivors and caregivers about using superheroes and villains as a means of recovery, more and more people questioned why I hadn't explored healing using Wonder Woman. Even my eighth-grade students asked why I had Wonder Woman comics in my class library but had not read them. Soon, I began to question this myself. Whether it was fate or respect for the first female superhero, I had all the material needed to research and write *How to Save Your Inner Wonder Woman* at my fingertips. This meant that when beginning to speak with my good friend, Dr. Michael Gomez, about using Wonder Woman to explore secondary traumatic stress in caregivers, much of the material needed to understand Wonder Woman's legacy was ready and waiting.

I began by reading *Wonder Woman: A Celebration of 75 Years* to get a feel for how the character has evolved over the years. From there I read George Perez's reimagining of Wonder Woman's origin in *Wonder Woman #1* "Gods and Mortals" (1987), continuing into the *New 52*, before ending with *DC Rebirth*. Needless to say, a lot of comics were consumed from a number of different authors. Many were amazing; others were . . . not. However, as Wonder Woman comics began to accumulate like stalagmites throughout the floor of my office, I began to understand why she has endured as a beloved superhero for nearly eighty years.

It's often said that if you want to solve a crime, call Batman. If you want to stop an alien invasion, call Superman. But if you want to end a war, call Wonder Woman. After researching and writing *How to Kill Your Batman*, *How to Master Your Inner Superman*, and *How to Save Your Inner Wonder Woman*, I now understand why. Diana Prince is more than a superpowered Amazon warrior with the ability to deflect bullets and fly in an invisible plane (sometimes) to stop bad guys. She is also an ambassador of Themyscira who makes it her priority to inform the world of the Amazon way of living as a means of instilling peace. Diana battles as a final recourse when negotiations have failed. She is strategic in her battle plans in a way that accounts for all the pieces on a board, positive and negative. However, more than that, she's compassionate, loving, and patient in a way that is unequaled by any hero in the DC or Marvel universes. Each punch she throws is calculated and made in an attempt to end violence, providing a path toward redemption for even the most heinous villains.

While Wonder Woman has boundless compassion, she is not naïve. Diana Prince is a character who knows that sometimes battles must be fought, but she never stops believing humanity has the potential to change for the better. As I write these words in the midst of a worldwide pandemic of COVID-19, reassurance, compassion, and love in the form of a powerful woman who happens to also be an Amazon warrior princess is precisely what the world needs during these traumatic and uncertain times.

Who Is Wonder Woman

Wonder Woman is a DC comic superhero developed by psychiatrist William Marston. Born Diana (later named Diana Prince), she first appeared in 1941 in *All-Star Comics* #8,

"Introducing Wonder Woman." In her original origin story, Diana was formed from clay by her mother, Hippolyta, queen of the Amazons, on an all-female island of warriors known as Paradise Island (later renamed Themyscira). She was given life by the Greek gods and raised to be an Amazon warrior in the same manner as her sisters. After the crash landing of Captain Steve Trevor of the US Army, Diana entered and won the competition to determine the Amazon champion who would leave Paradise Island and enter "man's world" to battle evil as Wonder Woman, never to return.

Over the nearly eighty years of Wonder Woman's existence, Diana's origins have somewhat changed, but much has remained the same. There has always been a connection to Greek gods and mythology in some way, shape, or form. Over the years, her weapons and clothes have changed to match the current generation's values, but her most-used and memorable weapons have always been her bullet deflecting Bracelets of Submission and her golden-truth lasso known as the "Perfect."

Is This Book for Me?

This guide was written with the intention of helping professional caregivers and allies of survivors of childhood sexual abuse such as (but not limited to):

- Counselors
- Therapists
- Psychiatrists
- Social workers
- Advocates
- Teachers
- First responders
- Child Protective Service workers
- Spouses/partners of survivors

- Love ones of survivors

who are battling **burnout, compassion fatigue**, and **secondary trauma stress**. All three are similar, but they differ in their effects on the mental well-being of caregivers.

Burnout is commonly a product of overwork by caregivers such as counselors, therapists, psychiatrists, and first responders. It happens over time due to continuous exposure to the trauma of others. It is specific to an individual's work culture and the practices of a workplace environment. If not addressed, it increases the risk for compassion fatigue.

Compassion Fatigue is not an immediate response to trauma exposure. Similar to burnout, it happens over time. Compassion fatigue can be experienced by all caregivers, first responders, and loved ones of survivors who care for others experiencing trauma or emotionally challenging conditions.

Secondary Traumatic Stress is triggered by direct or indirect exposure to trauma. Although the symptoms of secondary trauma are similar to post-traumatic stress disorder (such as dissociation, nightmares, depression, and anxiety) it does not meet the full criteria for PTSD.

How to Save Your Inner Wonder Woman is a guide that is meant to help those who have made it their mission to help survivors recover from sexual abuse trauma learn to practice trauma stewardship to ensure maintaining the health of *their* mental well-being. This guide is not *about* Wonder Woman. Instead, it uses Wonder Woman as a metaphor to assist in understanding the complexities of taking on the monumental task of helping survivors heal from childhood sexual abuse. As a reader, you do not have to know the evolution of Wonder Woman as a character throughout the DC universe in her seventy-nine years of existence. What is needed to be understood about Wonder Woman is explained in a way that is easy to follow and comprehend.

The Caregiver's Journey

To understand the path of trauma stewardship outlined throughout *How to Save Your Inner Wonder Woman*, Joseph Campbell's journey of a hero in relation to the hero Wonder Woman is used to understand **the healing journey of a caregiver**. In Joseph Campbell's 1949 book, *The Hero with A Thousand Faces*, the author explores the similarities of hero myths across the world and throughout the ages. Throughout his exploration in the book, he makes the argument that all heroes have the same defining characteristics that mark the progression of their voyage called the "hero's journey." This progressional voyage of the hero can be mapped step by step in the stories of Jesus, *Harry Potter*, and even *Star Wars*. This guide uses a similar version of Joseph Campbell's hero's journey and Wonder Woman to explain the path caregivers undertake when seeking to help to heal survivors of sexual abuse while maintaining the well-being of their own mental health. The steps of the healing journey of a caregiver are:

1) **The Call to Adventure**: The caregiver is called to help others heal from their traumatic past. In the first part of *How to Save Your Inner Wonder Woman*, this is referred to as "Leaving Your Paradise Island." During this step, the caregiver acquires and learns to use the tools needed to help survivors heal.

2) **Road of Trials:** The caregiver begins the process of helping survivors heal. During this step, helping others heal from their traumatic past begins to take its toll on the mental and emotional well-being of the caregiver.

3) **Apotheosis:** The high point when all is well. The caregiver achieves an "ah-ha" moment in understanding their journey toward healing others and themselves.

4) **Abyss:** The caregiver begins to notice there is a problem in the way they help survivors heal. Their mood becomes darker, and their outlook on why they help others begins to change due to burnout, compassion fatigue, or secondary traumatic stress.

5) **Belly of the Whale:** Similar to the decision to heal in the healing process of the survivor, caregivers reach a similar conclusion when deciding to practice trauma stewardship, in an attempt to maintain balance between their life, relationships, mental health, and their role as a caregiver.

6) **Crossing the First Thresholds:** The caregiver begins the process of identifying, understanding, and healing from the effects of burnout, compassion fatigue, and secondary traumatic stress.

7) **Atonement:** The caregiver learns from their past mistakes, forgives themselves of any perceived or real mistakes, and becomes stronger when learning to identify their own shortcomings and lean on others for support when needed.

8) **Master of Two Worlds:** Balance is achieved. The caregiver is able to balance work, relationships, and their personal activities in a way that is beneficial to help survivors heal and maintain their sense of mental well-being.

Throughout classic literature, the hero's journey is designed to be linear, progressing from beginning to end in a perfect arc. Unfortunately, life is not linear. There is no perfect arc that builds toward a dramatic climax before progressing toward a well-crafted and meaningful resolution. Instead, the healing journey of a caregiver is messy. Sometimes, the climax occurs before the rising action, or life's lessons never reach resolution.

The hero's journey of a caregiver is cyclical in nature, similar to the healing process of survivors of childhood sexual abuse. A step on the path of the caregiver's journey does not have to be experienced in a particular order before progressing to the next step in the process. Instead, the caregiver's journey is experienced out of order. Steps are often revisited numerous times at different stages throughout the journey of the caregiver, offering new insight and growth into how to help survivors heal while maintaining balance in their own life and mental well-being.

When reading this guide, it is important to take your time. There is no need to rush through the material. If one chapter seems critical to your journey as a caregiver, read that chapter first. If a particular section if too difficult, stop reading. Rest and reflect on the lessons you are learning. Revisit past chapters later in your journey to offer growth and insight that may have been forgotten, or for guidance about how to help others progress along their path. Above all else, be kind to yourself as you seek to save your inner Wonder Woman in the same way you would be kind to those you seek to help heal from their childhood trauma.

Writing as a Male Survivor of Childhood Sexual Abuse

I am a male survivor of childhood sexual abuse. It is for this reason that my guides *Heroes, Villains, and Healing, How to Kill Your Batman*, and *How to Master Your Inner Superman* have been written for male survivors. My history as a survivor offers me a unique lens in which to understand the effects of complex post-traumatic stress disorder (C-PTSD) and childhood sexual abuse on the perception of masculinity. I also write for male survivors because male survivors of sexual abuse are often ignored and made to believe they do not exist. Writing specifically for male survivors helps to foster a safe community for them to be recognized throughout society.

However, throughout this guide, there was an attempt made to not limit the message and resources for caregivers, first responders, partners, spouses, and love ones of male survivors. This guide attempts to help those who assist *all* survivors of childhood sexual abuse. That being said, it is important to know that I may sometimes be limited in my view of healing and helping other survivors. I am not a psychiatrist, therapist, or counselor for trauma of sexual abuse. I am a writer, secondary educator, father, husband, and male survivor of childhood sexual abuse who made the decision to heal and the choice to help other survivors know they are not as alone. For any shortcomings that may appear throughout this guide about how to help both male and female survivors, I humbly ask your forgiveness. It was not done out of malice, but rather a lack of knowledge. My wife, certain members of my family, close friends, therapists, and psychiatrists have helped me along the journey of my recovery. It is for them that I write this book.

Why Write for Caregivers of Childhood Sexual Abuse

Childhood sexual abuse has extensive ramifications that extend beyond adolescence and into adulthood, affecting the lives of survivors and many others as they work to build relationships. The effects of sexual abuse and assault can be detrimental to a survivor's mental, physical, and emotional health, causing feelings of depression and anxiety due to post-traumatic stress disorder (PTSD). Although this is true, healing for survivors of childhood sexual abuse is sometimes more difficult due to the effects on the development of a child's brain following the impact of suffering C-PTSD. C-PTSD has a longer lasting effect on survivors than PTSD. This is because the trauma of sexual abuse occurs early in the development of an individual's mental and social development, making it difficult to build lasting and trusting relationships with others.

Each year, millions of individuals are sexually abused, assaulted, and raped throughout the United States. While it is devastating to believe that many of these individuals will develop PTSD, what is more mind-boggling is that of those millions who will be victimized, sixty thousand will be children, with those aged 12-34 having the highest risk of sexual assault or rape, according to the United States Department of Health and Human Services. This means that each year, sixty thousand children could potentially develop C-PTSD. Research on sexual abuse, assault, and rape of children by the *Journal of the American Medical Association* in 2019 found that over 3.3 million women stated that their first sexual experience was rape. This means that one in sixteen women stated that their first act of sexual intercourse was forced or coerced, with many stating that it occurred as early as fifteen years old. *JAMA Pediatrics* also found in 2019 that the number of adolescents admitted to the emergency room for injuries related to sexual assault increased from 2,280 in 2010 to 5,058 in 2016.

The #MeToo movement has begun to bring the impact of sexual assault and rape of adult women from the shadows of our society into the light of harsh reality, but the truth of childhood sexual abuse is much bleaker. Statistics from the National Sexual Violence Resource Center's 2015 Data Debrief revealed that one in five women will be the victim of an attempted or completed rape in their lifetime, and one in fourteen men are forced against their will to penetrate another individual at some point in their lifetime. While these statistics are startling, it is important to remember that these statistics are not simply numbers in a report but young people who have been victimized as children.

Individuals who are the victims of childhood sexual abuse, assault, and rape who do not make the decision to heal grow up to be mothers, fathers, coworkers, classmates, and lovers who have the possibility of shedding the negative effects of their victimization on others. These survivors have individuals who care for and depend on their mental, physical, and emotional well-being. These loved ones may have witnessed the depression, anxiety, coping mechanisms, and self-destructive tendencies of a survivor and understand that healing from childhood sexual abuse is difficult, but they may not know how best to help. It is my hope that this guide can provide insight into what they can do to help as a partner, spouse, or family member if the person they love is being triggered by memories of past sexual abuse. As a male survivor of childhood sexual abuse, I have witnessed by wife, Sarah, struggle in knowing what to do to help me along my journey as a survivor. I write this guide with her in mind, hoping others can gain strength from our lessons as a couple as we both work to heal the effects of childhood trauma.

This guide is also meant to help professional caregivers who put the needs of trauma-impacted individuals before their own. While these individuals may view themselves, and be viewed by others, as superheroes, they are still human. These caregivers can become overwhelmed, suffering from depression and anxiety of their own due to the nature of their job, the same as anyone else. Using Wonder Woman as an extended metaphor throughout *How to Save Your Inner Wonder Woman*, I encourage these caregivers to practice self-care in order to reduce the possibility of burnout, compassion fatigue, and secondary traumatic stress. Practicing trauma stewardship is the only way to ensure caregivers do not become the villains of their own story.

Part One
Birth of Your Wonder Woman: Understanding the Meaning Behind Your Actions as a Caregiver

"As before, an Amazon will represent us in the outer world—set forth with the task of representing us and spreading our highest ideals. The notions of peaceful coexistence, of equality, of love and respect. This Amazon truly is the very best our nation has to offer."

—**Philippus**, *Wonder Woman #177*, "Paradise Found" (2002)

In the 2007 graphic novel *Justice*, written by Alex Ross and Jim Krueger, the secret identities of the superpowered group of heroes known as the Justice League have been discovered. The Legion of Doom, a group of villains comprised of the worst enemies of the Justice League, attack the mild-mannered identities of Clark Kent, Bruce Wayne, Barry Allen, and various other members of the league rather than their superhero alter egos. Although the world knows that Diana Prince is also Wonder Woman, she is no exception. The Amazonian princess is viciously attacked by her once friend and now enemy, Priscilla Rich (Cheetah). In the midst of battle, Wonder Woman recounts how she was chosen to be the Amazon's ambassador to the world. She thinks to herself:

The first name I ever knew was "daughter." I remember my mother holding me in the dawn. I remember the sea. And I remember her telling me that I was a gift. And that I was beautiful. My mother never wanted me to leave her, never wanted me to become the Amazon ambassador to the world. There was a contest among the Amazons, a test of endurance and wisdom, to see who would become Wonder Woman. It was forbidden for me to enter. She just never wanted me to be hurt. So, I wore a mask. I disguised myself and won the contest. And hurt my mother with my betrayal. I swore I'd never wear a mask again.

The battle between the heroine and Cheetah ends with Wonder Woman's face scarred by the villain's poisoned claws, causing Diana to return to her origins of clay when she was formed on the shores of Themyscira and blessed with life by the Greek gods. By the end of the novel, the poison of Cheetah's claws course through Wonder Woman's veins, baking her flesh from the inside out and leaving the heroine a hollow husk of ash and rock.

Ross and Krueger's depiction of Wonder Woman in *Justice* reminds readers that on the path toward becoming a hero, there is always an origin. No individual, fictional or otherwise, begins fully developed and in control of their lives. There is a progression of growth that ensures the creation of a dynamic character capable of feeling and expressing a full spectrum of emotions. Joseph Campbell explains in *Hero with a Thousand Faces* that theses first steps in a character's journey toward becoming a hero is known as the **Call to Adventure.** This is when a character departs from their home to places unknown to begin their adventure as a hero. In many ways, the healing journey of a caregiver beginning to help survivors heal from their childhood trauma is similar to Wonder Woman's account of her Call to Adventure in *Justice.*

Wonder Woman's words also allows readers to understand that being called to adventure also means being called to do battle, whether or not it is anticipated—battles that, no matter how well they are fought, inevitably lead to physical, emotional, or psychological scars. It is for this reason it is the job of caregivers to practice trauma stewardship to ensure the battle scars acquired while helping others heal do not remain open wounds. Similar to the way in which Diana burned from the inside out when unable to rid herself of Cheetah's poison, if wounds acquired by caregivers are left unhealed and allowed to fester, caregivers have the potential to become a shell of their former selves.

In this first part of *How to Save Your Inner Wonder Woman*, you will be asked to explore your own origins as a caregiver, first responder, or loved one of a survivor, and your choice to take on the task of leaving your Paradise Island to become a warrior to help others heal.

Chapter One
Leaving Paradise Island

"What if my destiny is waiting for me somewhere beyond the shores of paradise?"

—**Diana Prince**, *Wonder Woman #750,* "To Leave Paradise" (2020)

Wonder Woman was first molded into creation in 1941 by psychiatrist William Marston in *All-Star Comics #8*, "Introducing Wonder Woman." There is much that is different between the Diana Prince of the past and the heroine of the present. Due to the conservative nature of the 1940s, her clothing was much more reserved, revealing less skin in her long blue skirt speckled with white stars. In the past, there was no golden lasso, no invisible plane, and the Amazon princes was unable to take to the skies in the same manner as Superman.

Although much has changed over the years, there is still much that is the same between Marston's Diana Prince and the Wonder Woman of Greg Rucka in the DC Comics 2016 event, *Rebirth*. Wonder Woman has always had a connection to the gods of Greek mythology. Diana has always worn the bullet defecting Bracelets of Submission of the all-female Amazon warriors of Themyscira, and Captain Steve Trevor's crash landing on Themyscira has always been the catalyst that propels Diana to answer her call to adventure, leave Paradise Island forever, and become the Amazonian champion and ambassador to the world as Wonder Woman.

When Trevor crash lands on Themyscira (also known as Paradise Island), the hidden island of the Amazon warriors, in *All-Star Comics #8*, Diana is drawn to the army captain and the world of men. In true story-telling fashion of the 1940s, she even tells her mother, Hippolyta, queen of the Amazons, that she loves him after seeing his face only once. Using the Magic Sphere (a large disc given to the Amazons by the Greek goddess Athena, allowing the viewer to witness what has happened, is happening, and will happen in the world of man), Diana and Hippolyta watch Trevor's past actions as if watching a television. They discover Steve's mission to save American lives that resulted in his crash landing on Themyscira.

Afterward, when the Magic Sphere reveals what it can of Trevor's past, Diana knows for certain that she must help the pilot get home to complete his mission of defeating evil. Hippolyta also now knows Trevor must be assisted in his fight against evil after being visited by the spirits of the goddesses Aphrodite and Athena, who tell the queen, "The gods have decreed that this American Army officer crash on Paradise Island. You must deliver him back to America—to help fight the forces of hate and oppression . . . You must send him with your strongest and wisest Amazon, the finest of your Wonder Women."

Hippolyta refuses to allow Diana to enter the competition to determine the Amazon champion. However, against the wishes of her mother, Diana disguises herself behind a mask, enters the tournament, and becomes the Amazonian champion. Crowned with a golden tiara, and a red girdle with a golden bird and outstretched wings upon the breast plate, Diana is named Wonder Woman. Afterward, she leaves Paradise Island with Steve Trevor, not knowing if she will ever return to the place of her birth.

In Marston's origin of Wonder Woman, Diana Prince leaves Paradise Island, an island of perfection and immortality, to enter the world of men to battle evil. Through the eyes of readers of this 1941 comic then and now, Diana did something heroic, selfless, and noble. She made the choice to forgo her immortality and life of perfection in order to devote her life to the service of others as the Amazonian warrior champion and world ambassador. As a caregiver, you may see pieces of yourself and your own actions in those of Diana as she begins her journey on the road to becoming Wonder Woman. Seeing others in need of help in the same way Diana sees the problems of the world of men in the Magic Sphere, you may have made the choice to enter your own tournament of champions to leave Paradise Island, begin your Call to Adventure, and help others as a caregiver of survivors of childhood trauma begin healing their **adverse childhood experience (ACE)** of childhood sexual abuse.

Adverse Childhood Experiences and the ACE Study

Childhood sexual abuse is one of nine forms of adverse childhood experiences (ACEs) that have been linked to long-term physical and mental health complications in adults and adolescents. The study of the effects of adverse childhood experiences began when the Center for Disease Control and Kaiser Health Plan's Department of Prevention Medicine conducted the first ACE study in 1998. The experiment involved the cooperation of over seventeen thousand middle-aged, middle-class Americans who agreed to help researchers study nine categories of childhood abuse and household dysfunction:

1. Recurrent physical abuse
2. Recurrent emotional abuse
3. Contact sexual abuse
4. An alcoholic and/or drug abuser in the household
5. An incarcerated household member
6. A household member who is chronically depressed, mentally ill, institutionalized, or suicidal
7. Mother is treated violently
8. One or no parents
9. Emotional or physical neglect

The study found that as the number of ACE's increased, the risk for health problems increased as well. Health problems such as:

- Alcoholism and alcohol abuse
- Chronic obstructive pulmonary disease (COPD)
- Depression
- Fetal death
- Health-related quality of life
- Illicit drug use
- Ischemic heart disease (IHD)
- Liver disease
- Risk for intimate partner violence
- Multiple sexual partners
- Sexually transmitted diseases (STDs)
- Smoking
- Suicide attempts
- Unintended pregnancies
- Early initiation of smoking
- Early initiation of sexual activity
- Adolescent pregnancy

These health concerns revealed that ACEs have a strong impact on adult and adolescent health, substance abuse, sexual behavior, the risk of revictimization, and stability in relationships. It also revealed that the higher the ACE score, the greater the risk of things like heart disease, liver disease, HIV, and STDs. Individuals with six or more ACEs, compared to individuals with one or no ACEs, were found to have a twenty-year reduction in life expectancy.

Since the initial ACE study performed in 1998, research has expanded to include individuals of different cultural and racial backgrounds across all fifty states. Surveys were distributed to collect data pertaining to ACEs in 2003, 2007, and 2011/12. In

2016, the National Survey of Children's Health (NSCH) continued the ACE study by mailing surveys to parents and guardians with at least one child, asking a series of yes-or-no questions. Although the questions in this cycle of the survey still remained limited to no more than ten, they were slightly redesigned to include over 50,000 participants.

This study found remarkably similar yet startling results:

- Economic hardship and divorce or separation of a parent or guardian are the most common ACEs reported nationally in all states.

- Just under half (45 percent) of children in the United States have experienced at least one ACE.

- One in ten children nationally has experienced three or more ACEs, placing them in a category of especially high risk. In five states, as many as one in seven children had experienced three or more ACEs.

- Children of different races and ethnicities do not experience ACEs equally. Nationally, 61 percent of black non-Hispanic children and 51 percent of Hispanic children have experienced at least one ACE, compared with 40 percent of white non-Hispanic children and only 23 percent of Asian non-Hispanic children. In every division, the prevalence of ACEs is lowest among Asian non-Hispanic children and, in most divisions, is highest among black non-Hispanic children.

The 2016 cycle of the ACE study found that not only have ACEs become more prevalent throughout our society, but ACEs are not evenly shared by children in every state or of every race. Adverse childhood experiences can create toxic levels of stress, fear, terror, and helplessness, which can interrupt mental and physical development, creating cognitive distortions and an altered view of the world and themselves.

While the results of the 2016 cycle of the ACE study are troubling, the study also found that there are ways to prevent or lessen the negative effects of chronic and toxic stress created by ACEs. Individuals who have a strong understanding of their emotions and work to develop interpersonal skills were able to lessen the effects of ACEs on their mind and body. The study also found that having a positive, supportive relationship with one or more adults is one of the most important keys to buffering the effects of ACEs as a child or adolescent. This relationship does not have to be with one's parents, but it does have to be with an adult who cares and is supportive. This means, and helps to prove, that the key to fighting the effects of complex trauma is relationship building. For you as a caregiver or loved one of a survivor of childhood sexual abuse, this means your role in the healing process of survivors is invaluable when reducing the impact of ACEs.

The adverse childhood experience of sexual abuse and assault rips survivors from the comfort of feeling safe and in control of their body and their surroundings. As a caregiver, you may already recognize the impact you have in combatting adverse childhood experiences by building positive relationships with survivors in an attempt to help them heal from their childhood trauma. You may even view your actions as those of Wonder Woman, a hero willing to depart from the safety and security of their personal Paradise Island to help others help themselves heal. However, this is not true for all caregivers. Some caregivers may not view themselves as a hero in the battle to help survivors recover. Instead, they view their departure from Paradise Island as a choice dictated by forces beyond their control. Before determining where you settle on the spectrum of helping survivors of childhood sexual abuse, we must first define what it means to be a caregiver.

Leaving Paradise Island as a Caregiver

When Diana left Paradise Island with Steve Trevor, she made the selfless choice to become the Amazonian champion and ambassador, Wonder Woman, placing the needs of others before her own as the superhero. In many ways, professional caregivers are similar to Diana when making the choice to help individuals who have been impacted by the trauma of childhood sexual abuse. These caregivers include (but are not limited to):

- Counselors
- Therapists
- Psychiatrists
- Social workers
- Advocates
- Teachers
- First responders
- Child Protective Service workers

Some caregivers, such as therapists, social workers, and first responders, may have left their Paradise Island knowing they will encounter children and adult survivors who have experienced a number of adverse childhood experiences. They heard and answered their Call to Adventure as a caregiver. These individuals may have entered their profession knowing they may have to shoulder a portion of the pain harbored by their patients in order to help them heal as an unspoken rule of their career. These caregivers know that survivors of childhood sexual abuse were stripped from their island of perfection and sought to understand the strategies needed to help their patients move through the healing process to begin to recover from their childhood victimization.

However, some caregivers may enter their careers without knowing the different hats they may have to wear to understand the effects of childhood trauma and how to help others heal. These individuals may have left their Paradise Island under false pretenses, unknowing that they may also have to take on the job of counselor, social worker, and mentor along with the other listed requirements of their profession. Although many of these caregivers rise to the occasion of helping survivors as best they can, they are called on to take on the role of being an Amazon warrior without warning, causing some to eventually refuse the Call to Adventure due to burnout and compassion fatigue, which can occur in any caregiver regardless of their intentions when deciding to help others heal.

As a caregiver, although you may have never experienced trauma of your own, the constant exposure to the trauma of others has the possibility of leading to burnout, compassion fatigue, and secondary traumatic stress. This guide will help you apply the strategies of maintaining a healthy balance of life and work to heal yourself while helping others to heal themselves.

Leaving Paradise Island as a Loved One of a Survivor

You may not be reading this guide as a professional caregiver of the above listed professions. Instead, you may be the spouse, partner, or family member of a survivor of childhood sexual abuse seeking to find a way to help them heal. You may also be reading this guide in an attempt to understand how and what *you* should be feeling or doing when helping someone you care for heal from sexual abuse or assault.

While navigating through this guide and seeking to understand the thoughts and feelings of your loved one, it is important to know that the person you care for was forced to leave the safety and security of their own Paradise Island following the traumatization of their sexual abuse as a child. Unlike Diana who willingly entered the tournament of champions to become Wonder Woman, survivors were not given a choice to leave the safety of their childhood in order to become a hero. Instead, the comfort and happiness of being a *kid* was stripped away following their sexual abuse, forcing them to view the world through a lens of cognitive distortions and negative automatic thoughts. As a victim, they may have been:

- raped or otherwise penetrated
- forced to penetrate someone else
- made to watch sexual acts either in person or on pornographic videos
- forced to perform oral sex
- made to pose naked for an adult's gratification
- made to fondle another male or female against their will
- forced to take part in ritualized abuse which was physical, psychological, or sexual torture

However, as a survivor rather than a victim, they have chosen to not let their past define who they are as an individual. They, like you, choose to take on the role of being an Amazon warrior working to heal themselves and possibly others who were sexually victimized in a similar manner. This is the difference between remaining a victim and becoming a survivor. It means making the decision to recover from the sexual abuse of the past rather than deny and avoid its impact on the present.

Survivors are not the only ones who may have been stripped away from the perfection of their Paradise Island. As a loved one of a survivor of childhood sexual abuse, you may have also been stripped away from your island of perfection to become a warrior against your wishes. As a family member, you may have been surprised to learn the person you care for was sexually abused as a child. You may be filled with rage, guilt, remorse, confusion, and even skepticism about whether the sexual abuse actually occurred. The veil of a perfect relationship as a spouse or partner may suddenly be pulled away, causing you to question if you want to do battle to save your Wonder Woman or part ways. On the other hand, as a spouse or partner of a survivor of childhood sexual abuse, you may have entered into the relationship knowing the person you love was sexually abused as a child. Although this may be true, you may not fully know what it means to begin healing from childhood sexual abuse and how it will (or has) affected your relationship. All of these thoughts, feelings, and concerns are common and normal as you consider taking on the role of learning to defend and help the person you love begin the process of healing.

Beginning to heal from the complex post-traumatic stress disorder (C-PTSD) caused by childhood trauma cannot be accomplished alone. That being said, if you have made the choice to help a loved one heal from the trauma of childhood sexual abuse, thank you. This monumental task cannot be accomplished alone or in a vacuum. It is difficult and means putting in the work to recover as a survivor. This guide will help you to understand the healing process and your role in helping the survivor recover, but also how to maintain your mental health and setting of boundaries to reduce the possibility of developing compassion fatigue or secondary traumatic stress. Helping a loved one heal is a difficult task that is cyclical, continuous, but helpful in allowing you to understand, grow, and heal with your loved one as you both work toward saving your inner Wonder Woman.

Chapter Two
Trauma Mastery, Wonder Woman, and Cheetah

"I do, Steve, but I can't marry you until my services are no longer needed to battle crime and injustice! Only then can I think about myself."

—**Wonder Woman**, *Wonder Woman #99*, "Top Secret" (1958)

Diana was told by her mother, Queen Hippolyta, from the time of her birth, that she was made from clay and given life by the gods. In 2013's *Wonder Woman Volume #1*, "Blood," writer Brian Azzarello provides modern readers with a context for Wonder Woman's origins when Hermes, the messenger of the Greek gods, explains to Zola (a young woman carrying the illegitimate son of Zeus) the origins of the superhero. He tells her:

> *According to legend, Hippolyta—the queen—her womb was barren, yet she desperately wanted a child. So, on a moonless night, she fashioned a child of clay and prayed to the gods for a miracle. When she was done, she fell exhausted into a deep slumber. And with the sun above, Hippolyta was awakened by her child. Wonder Woman is the perfect Amazon—no male seed created her.*

As a child, Diana was taught the ways of being an Amazon and how the female warriors came to live on Themyscira. Although Diana knew the history of the Amazons and was consistently chastised by her teachers to appreciate and enjoy life on Paradise Island, she continued to feel a pull toward "man's world." It is for this reason when Steve Trevor crash lands on Themyscira and reveals that humanity needs help in its battle against evil, it appears to be ordained that Diana become Wonder Woman. However, is this the truth? Was Diana truly made from clay and chosen by the gods to fight evil as Wonder Woman, or is there an alternate truth to the heroine's origin?

Later in "Blood," Diana discovers the truth of her past, rocking the foundation of her view of herself as a hero, the meaning of family, and how she can move forward knowing the truth. Queen Hippolyta tells her daughter the truth of how she came into the world. She tells Diana that she was not made from clay. Instead, she was the result of an affair with Zeus. Hippolyta tells her daughter, "Diana, before there was you, there was a man. No. There was more than a man. There was a god. The god. There was Zeus." Hippolyta explains to Diana how the two were lovers, and Diana was a result of their affair. To keep Diana safe from Hera's wrath due to the infidelity of her husband (again), the lie of Diana's origin from clay began and was perpetuated by the queen and a few of her confidants.

After being told the truth, Diana feels betrayed, as if she is living a lie. She no longer believes she is allowed to call herself Wonder Woman, because she left Paradise Island under false pretenses. She no longer views her actions as truthful when attempting to show compassion to her enemies. Diana believes she cannot help others using the magic lasso to reveal the true intentions motivating their actions when she no longer knows the truth behind her own actions as Wonder Woman.

You, as a caregiver to a survivor of childhood sexual abuse, may have left your Paradise Island in an attempt to help others along their path of recovery without knowing the truth behind your actions. Similar to Wonder Woman, believing her yearning to be a part of man's world was ordained by the gods rather than her actually being a demigod, you may believe your actions to help survivors as selfless, when you may be masking the truth of your intentions behind a mask of **trauma mastery.**

Trauma Mastery

Sometimes, the motivations of a caregiver are due to a need to acquire **trauma mastery** over a traumatic event in their own past. In Laura van Dernoot Lipsky's guide, *Trauma Stewardship*, she explains how trauma mastery is what we as humans often do to reconcile a lack of control at some point in our lives. After experiencing a traumatic event, she explains how individuals "create and re-create situations as similar to the traumatic incident as possible. We seek to turn a traumatic situation in which we once felt powerless into a new situation where we feel competent and in charge." Many times, trauma mastery occurs when first encountering trauma that could not be prevented. Lipsky explains how trauma mastery takes root in three places:

1. **Our activities:** What is done when not working at a job or career.

2. **Our relationships:** The people chosen to spend and share our lives alongside.

3. **Our choice of work:** The profession chosen as worthy of our time and effort.

Trauma mastery may be the reason why you as a professional caregiver may have decided to be a counselor, therapist, first responder, or why you are in a relationship striving to help a survivor heal from their childhood trauma. As a caregiver, your experience with ACEs may be the driving force behind your actions, placing you in situations to re-experience the traumatic events of the past to regain control of a time you felt weak. To understand your connection to trauma mastery as a caregiver, you have to examine not only your past, but your present actions, relationships, and the driving force behind your chosen profession.

Wonder Woman can offer an understanding of how an inability to address the truth of trauma mastery can lead to a cycle of neglecting self-care resulting in burnout, compassion fatigue, or secondary traumatic stress. The beginning of Wonder Woman's development of her trauma mastery can be demonstrated in Diana's first failure on her Road of Trials as a hero and the inability to save her friend, Dr. Barbara Ann Minerva, from transforming into the villain, Cheetah.

The Curse of the Cheetah and Crossing the First Threshold

In the 2016 DC Comics event, *Rebirth*, writer Greg Rucka reimagines the origin of Wonder Woman and her relationship to the villain, Cheetah. Over the eighty years of Wonder Woman's existence, the alter ego of Cheetah has been a number of characters. In the Gold and Silver Age of Comics, she was Priscilla Rich. During the Bronze Age, she was Deborah Domaine, and now the character is currently embodied by Dr. Barbara Ann Minerva. Not only in Rucka's reimaging of the character, but in other reincarnations as well, Wonder Woman and Cheetah were once close friends.

In *Wonder Woman #1-25* (2016-17), Greg Rucka creates an alternating cycle of comics that revisit Diana's past while on Themyscira and her journey as a hero across the first threshold while addressing her actions in the present as Wonder Woman. The odd-numbered comics address Diana's journey toward discovering the truth of her past and why she can no longer return to the island of her birth, Themyscira. These twenty-five comics are amazingly written and drawn, providing readers with an exceptional context for understanding Wonder Woman's complicated relationship with Dr. Barbara Ann Minerva, how Barbara Ann becomes Cheetah, and a context for understanding the possible development of your own trauma mastery as a caregiver through the lens of Wonder Woman's need to heal villains who appear irredeemable.

Wonder Woman #8, "Interlude" (2016), provides readers with the origin of Dr. Minerva. The comic explains how Barbara Ann spent her childhood pretending to be an Amazon princess while being told by her no-nonsense father to put away childish things and become an adult. Later, as an adult, she studies ancient Greek, researches the origin of the Amazon culture, and journeys on an expedition to discover the location of Themyscira. However, this is not when Diana and Barbara Ann meet for the first time. They meet for the first time when Dr. Minerva (who is an expert in ancient Greek linguistics and culture) is called in by the United States government to translate what Diana is saying after first appearing on American soil with Captain Steve Trevor.

Wonder Woman # 16, "God Watch: Part One" (2017), and *Wonder Woman #18*, "God Watch: Part Two" (2017), provide readers with a montage of the development of Barbara Ann and Diana's friendship. During these first few years, Diana provides Barbara Ann with information about the Amazons and how they came to live on Themyscira, while Barbara Ann teaches Diana about the ins and outs of man's world. Unfortunately, the more Diana tells Barbara Ann about Themyscira and the Amazon's connection to the Greek gods and goddesses, the more she becomes obsessed with the possibility of the existence of other gods.

Convinced she has discovered the location of the ancient god Urkartaga, Barbara Ann takes an expedition into the heart of the rain forest to discover its location. Afraid for the life of her friend, Diana attempts to convince her to not go, explaining how ancient gods are dangerous and cannot be trusted. Unable to convince Barbara Ann not to go, Diana gives Dr. Minerva a tracking device that, if in trouble, would send Wonder Woman a signal to help no matter where she was on earth. Unfortunately, the device did not work, and when Diana realizes she has not heard from her friend in a number of weeks, it is too late. Dr. Barbara Ann Minerva has already transformed into Cheetah and been cursed by Urkartaga to crave and eat "man flesh."

Over her years as a hero, Wonder Woman battles Cheetah while Diana also attempts to resurrect her friend Barbara Ann, who she knows is hidden inside. Unfortunately, no matter how hard she tries, she always fails and Barbara Ann remains Cheetah. It is because of Diana's failure to save Barbara Ann that she continuously attempts to reform villains whose actions appear irredeemable. Diana's need for trauma mastery is why she would not give up attempting to reform villains such as Mayfly and Silver Swan (discussed in "Part Two: Becoming a Hero") when all hope seems lost on their reformation.

Diana and Wonder Woman refuse to give up their need to show and have compassion for others, no matter what mistakes they may have made in the past. She has to believe that even the most heinous villains can be reformed. If she does not hold true to this belief, she loses hope for Barbara Ann, viewing her inability to save her friend as a sign of her weakness and shortcomings as a hero.

As a caregiver, you may view your actions in the same manner as Wonder Woman, due to a similar traumatic incident in your past that may have been out of your control. The inability to help yourself or others escape a traumatic situation may have made you feel weak in the same way Diana feels weak each time she cannot save Barbara Ann. Your inability to process and move on from your traumatic past may be why you choose to help survivors heal. Your ability to practice trauma mastery allows control over your *activities* as a part-time volunteer for a survivor's hotline, your *relationship* with a survivor as a partner or family member, or your choice of *work* as a counselor, therapist, psychiatrist, psychologist, social worker, or first responder.

If you practice trauma mastery as a caregiver, you may have a sense that your work is high stakes. It is because of this sense of all-or-nothing, and that your job may be the difference between life and death for a survivor, that you see the need to sacrifice pieces of yourself when helping survivors heal. Unfortunately, practicing trauma mastery as a caregiver or loved one for a survivor leaves the possibility that you may suffer battle wounds in order to help them heal. When you are unable to process or understand your trauma mastery, it can lead to burnout, compassion fatigue, or secondary traumatic stress as you place more pressure on yourself as a caregiver to *save* survivors rather than *help* them understand how to heal themselves.

Chapter Three
Leaving My Paradise Island
(Autobiographical)

"They say I have been so many things to them I never meant to be. But I am grateful all the same."

—**Wonder Woman**, *Wonder Woman #750*, "To Me" (2020)

Journaling has always been a part of my healing process. As a child, I consistently wrote about my thoughts on love, relationships, life, and trauma. Writing has always provided me an escape toward understanding myself and others. This first autobiographical chapter explains my exit from the Paradise Island of my childhood and the creation of my trauma mastery in an attempt to cope with the adverse childhood experience of my childhood sexual abuse. This chapter also includes the thoughts of my wife, Sarah, as she helped guide me toward the path of healing rather than coping with the trauma of my childhood trauma in adverse ways. This is done to help caregivers and survivors know that healing cannot be accomplished alone. Without Sarah's guidance, this book (and all the others) would never have been written. She explains how, similar to Wonder Woman, she answered the call to help me battle my demons, leaving her Paradise Island to become my Wonder Woman.

Kenny

I am a male survivor of childhood sexual abuse. At eight years old, I was sexually assaulted by my thirteen-year-old sister. For two years, while my parents believed I was being babysat while they went to work, or spent time with one another, friends, and family, I was being groomed through the use of pornographic videos and raped in the basement of our home. In my memoir, *Raped Black Male*, I explain how for two years the sexual assault continued, until one day, after church, she told me, "We can't do that anymore. It never happened, and if you tell anyone, you'll get in trouble." Afterward, I was confused, angry, and lived in a constant state of fear. For over twenty years of my life, I kept this secret hidden away and worked at building an armor of protection in the form of perfectionism, hypervigilance, workaholism, and humor in an attempt to feel safe.

On the outside, I lived under the façade of perfection. On the inside, I felt like anything but a hero as I battled anxiety and depression while attending Peoria High School, college at Bowling Green State University, and into my career as a secondary educator in Baltimore, Maryland.

After marrying Sarah and moving to Baltimore, the trauma of being raped as a child began to take its toll on my mental health. I remember morning panic attacks that would leave me incapacitated on the floor of the bathroom of our two-bedroom apartment, crying and repeating, "I'm fine. I'm fine. I'm fine." Sarah would hold me in her arms, attempting to stop my body from violently shaking. Those mornings, I would force myself to put on dress pants, a button-up shirt, tie, dress shoes, and walk out the door to teach at-risk boys and girls who looked like me.

At the time, there were numerous reasons to not give up as a secondary educator. Although the job was difficult, I believed it was my responsibility as a husband for my newly formed family of choice to stick it out, no matter how difficult it was to work. Second, as a male teacher of color who suffered from the effects of an adverse childhood, I knew the high stakes of my job. I knew there was a necessity to be at school every day with an engaging lesson and a safe learning environment, because for most of my students, school was the only respite they had from a society that viewed them as an adult when they were only an eighth-grade student. School was their opportunity to eat a (usually) healthy breakfast and lunch. It also provided students with the opportunity to succeed, fail, and act with the carefree nature that should be the right of every child, rather than the responsibility of being the man of the house. These thoughts are what developed my attempt to master my own childhood trauma.

At the end of the workday, I would return home exhausted but also relaxed, knowing that for at least a few hours, the pressure of needing to perform the role of a man who had it all together could be locked away until the new day. At the time, I was in denial of my poor mental health and panic attacks from the previous morning. Sarah would attempt to coax me into discussing the severity of the previous morning, but I would refuse, claiming, "Everything's fine. I'm fine." Instead of discussing my emotions, I would visit the gym to relieve accumulated stress and anxiety. The lifting of weights and running on the treadmill would succeed in making me numb until the next morning when the cycle began again.

This was the cycle for the better part of the first years of our marriage. Over time, Sarah began insisting I visit a therapist. Rather than agree, I insisted we did not have enough time or money. To calm her down, I would say, "I'll find one over the summer, I promise." A promise that was never fulfilled, because with the heat of summer came the relaxation every teacher strives to reach throughout the haze of standardized tests, SLO's, lesson plans, and parent-teacher conferences. For three months, the panic attacks would subside. The necessity of needing to relieve accumulated anxiety through the incessant running of miles on the treadmill would be no more, making the need for a therapist obsolete—that is, until the approach of September and the beginning of a new academic year.

For three years, I lived in a state of denial, perfection, hypervigilance, and workaholism that placed more strain than necessary on our marriage, causing my mental health to decline until it completely collapsed shortly after the purchase of our first home, the completion of my master's degree in education from Johns Hopkins University, and the birth of my daughter, Mirus.

As a child, I was sexually assaulted by my sister from the age of eight until I was ten, the victim of the domestic abuse and alcoholism of my father, and homeless following the foreclosure of my childhood home, all before the age of eighteen. Since then, I lived in a state of fear, coping with my childhood trauma rather than healing from it. This is because healing cannot take place in an unsafe environment. The uncertainty of my future as a college student and young adult caused me to exhaust my energy while attempting to survive. However, in 2013, that all changed. The purchase of our first home and a career that provided a livable salary made it possible to address the adverse childhood experiences of my past, and Mirus ensured I no longer lived in a state of denial.

With Mirus's birth, there was no longer time available to spend hours in the gym numbing my emotions, afternoons lying in bed battling depression, or mornings on the bathroom floor battling severe anxiety about the unpredictability of teaching a new unit to loving (but very difficult) class of teenagers. Mirus needed to be fed, changed, bathed, rocked to sleep, entertained, and loved. Sarah, who is also an educator, had her own lessons to teach on top of the responsibilities of being a mother. Placing more pressure on our marriage due to my trauma and mental illness was not an option, but rather than talk about my emotions and seek help from a therapist, I suffered a mental breakdown.

Severe depression and thoughts of suicide left me unable to get out of bed. Unable to be ignored any longer, Sarah's support guided me towards finding a therapist, getting on medication, and beginning the process of healing from my childhood sexual abuse. Over the years, I have learned to communicate with Sarah about how I am feeling, and we both are better at communicating with the other about what we need. We learned to lean on one another following the loss of her younger brother, TJ; the passing of our son, Cassus; the infection of the pericardial sac around my heart resulting in a viral heart infection; and stress-filled work environments leading to anxiety, burnout, and compassion fatigue. This guide is meant to help people like my wife and Susan Todd, my therapist, who are the wonder women in the lives of so many others who are battling to recover from the traumas of their past. I hope they find the support needed to take care of themselves while also helping others to heal and grow.

Sarah

Like you, dear reader, leaving my island was an event that changed my life completely. However, how I came to brave new waters and places unknown may have been very different from your own experience. Some of you may have deliberately begun your journey as a choice. A path was laid in front of you, or you may be at the fork in the road now and are reading this book in your deliberations about how to proceed. I feel that I never had such an overt invitation, no outright Call to Adventure. As I stood on my island, I never noticed the tide moving in and the sands slowly receding under my feet. Each time I looked down, the shore seemed to shift farther and farther behind me, but I kept telling myself, "This is okay. I can still touch." Then, "It's still okay. I can still see the shore from here." Until one day, I looked up and realized that we were now out on the open water, with no assurance of solid footing and no point of reference upon the horizon to find our way back.

On that day, while I was at work, my husband called me to tell me that he was on his way to the hospital. He told me that after I had kissed him goodbye and left the house, he had not gone to work that day. Instead, he had sat at home and contemplated whether the brace above our bedroom closet door would hold his weight on the end of the belt with which he planned to hang himself. Fortunately, he had the blessed realization that he needed to call a family friend who was an EMT. I often silently thank God for that friend, that he answered his phone and came to our aid.

Like I said, this was the moment when I realized we were unmoored, in dangerous waters, seemingly lost, but there were the other moments leading up to this. Small waves came in, washing away more and more of my island, inch by inch, slowly sweeping me out to sea. And for me, these moments happened as I lived my life. I didn't choose it. They just happened, and they continued to happen in a slow, insistent way.

The smaller waves looked like the mornings that began at 4 a.m. with crippling panic attacks. I would wake and the bed would be shaking with the tremors of my husband's silent sobs. I didn't know what to do but to hold him, breathing as deeply as I could, trying to somehow will him to breathe.

Further back, our rare arguments were ended far too soon with the slamming of a door and hours-long disappearances. Then, once the anger subsided, Kenny would rarely agree to revisit those emotions, holding them at bay, denying and refusing that they had even existed.

Still further back to the night when we both realized where our relationship was headed—days before our first kiss—he told me about the abuse. Over a spaghetti dinner he had cooked for me as his opening salvo in our courtship, he told me that his sister had abused him for years in the basement of his childhood home. I think he knew that the foundations of our relationship would eventually be rocked to their core by this fact. He was giving me an out, even if he didn't know it, and I think I also knew what this moment was, and somewhere deep down, I guess I did make some sort of choice. I already loved him. He had been one of my closest and best friends. I chose to love him, though I did not know what that truly meant.

Prior to this moment, I did not know a lot about Kenny's past. I knew he had experienced a hard life from small quips and moments he shared over the three previous years I had known him. These were already small waves upon the water that should have let me know the coastline here was ever-changing. I often think that I should have been prepared for what was to come.

As friends, Kenny had mentioned growing up in a violent household, but only through small, joking tidbits. He had mentioned being homeless in his final years of high school, reminiscing about having a parent-free after-prom party in his empty, foreclosed-upon house, an empty house and a bunch of crazy high school kids having too much fun for their own good. I often think about how lonely that night must have been for him, surrounded by friends in the shell of his old life he could never get back.

I could often tell from his demeanor around some of our friends that something was not okay. Kenny was often the life of the party. He was so funny, so impossibly charming, caring, and emotive. People would be drawn to him. "What a great guy!" they would say. "Kenny is the absolute best!" His popularity often led to an expectation among our friends to rely on Kenny to perform—to inject life into our social gatherings, which I could tell would weigh on him. On some days, he would retreat into his headphones, silent. I would have to remind some of our friends to give him some space. He later told me he deeply appreciated this and came to love me for how I protected him in those small ways. In a way, I was already becoming a Wonder Woman without knowing.

Like me, dear reader, you may have had these same flashes of truth that unavoidably rise up to meet you as you begin to know the survivor(s) with which you are becoming closer. When we were just friends, these small clues began to add up. When we became partners, our increasing intimacy uncovered new levels of trauma that had lurked beneath the surface. You may have your own versions of these small, accumulating waves growing in strength. They can be met with dread, with ignorance (like me), or be recognized and accepted for what they are.

I look back now on that day of absolute terror—the day I got the call from Kenny as he rode to the hospital—with much different emotions than the ones I felt on that day. The slow-moving tsunami of intermittent panic attacks and emotional outbursts and disassociation had filled me to the brim with dread and isolation, and I hadn't even realized it. The dam broke that day, and while I am not one to panic when events like this happen, inside I was an explosion of terror. Now, I look back and I see a pivotal moment. In this moment, when we were truly adrift, we were forced to chart a course *toward something*. No more drifting without direction, letting the waves push us from one place to another. We began to chart a course toward a place where we were both no longer lost but could stand together on dry land.

I love my husband beyond anything I can describe to you, dear reader, but that does not provide me some magical power or rare noble quality. I can easily imagine a world where no matter how much I loved my husband, our story could have ended tragically. I cannot give you any answers as to why it did not. But I am confident, dear reader, that in every universe, these events were still going to happen. There was no possibility that I could stay on my island forever. In every one of our stories, I always have to leave the island. Kenny's abuse happened, which means the act of loving my husband meant leaving the island must also happen. In some stories, I imagine myself braver and more sure. In some, I imagine myself handling things worse, but no matter what, I still have to leave the island. I cannot stay, because while the trauma are the waves washing my island away, our love was the current gently pulling me where I eventually needed to go. Just as Kenny's recovery has become a pivotal part of his life's journey, becoming his Wonder Woman was a guiding current in mine.

Part Two
Becoming a Hero: Helping Others Heal from Childhood Sexual Abuse

"I have seen all I have been to others. What I am to myself? I do this because I am this. I hope that is enough."

—**Wonder Woman**, *Wonder Woman #750*, "To Me" (2020)

A teenaged Diana Prince of Themyscira is tasked with finding the separate pieces needed to assemble the future costume of Wonder Woman. First, Hippolyta provides her daughter with a clue directing her into the ocean off the coast of Paradise Island. Once in the water, Diana notices the first piece of her costume, the white stars of her skirt. Unfortunately, they are inside a giant clam that snaps shut each time she gets close. Using a large piece of coral, Diana devises a plan. Sharpening the coral's end to a point, she props open the mouth of the giant clam, enters, and retrieves the white stars, which she places on the blue fabric of her long skirt.

Next, Diana swims to Volcano Island to retrieve the second, and possibly most important, piece of her costume, her truth-telling golden lasso. After climbing to the summit of the volcano at the center of the island, Wonder Girl ventures into its molten core, where she spots and retrieves the Perfect.

Finally, using the updraft caused by the volcanic heat of the lava and the cool surrounding air, Diana glides into the air. Once in the sky, Diana spots a giant bird and quickly devises a plan to retrieve the third and final piece of her Wonder Woman costume, the golden eagle attached to the breast plate of her girdle. Diana ties the golden lasso around the giant claws of the bird, hitching a ride to the bird's nest. Once in the nest of the giant bird, Diana retrieves the golden eagle emblem among the sticks and twigs of the bird's eggs.

Following the completion of her trials as Wonder Girl, she returns to Themyscira, where Hippolyta declares to the island that her daughter is worthy to one day wear the costume of Wonder Woman.

This story from *Wonder Woman #107,* "Wonder Woman Amazon Teen-Ager" (1968), helps to demonstrate Diana's **Road of Trials** as a superhero. Joseph Campbell explains in *Hero of a Thousand Faces* how the Road of Trials must be accomplished by every hero before being considered worthy of being called a hero. It is during the Road of Trials that risks are taken, mistakes are made, and experience is gained during the many trials of the hero's adventures. While the Road of Trials is filled with mistakes and the accumulation of scars, it is also accompanied with the gaining of wisdom. The difficult lessons learned as a result of venturing down the Road of Trials is not only true for heroes, but caregivers as well. Unfortunately, the wisdom gained during the Road of Trials along the healing journey of a caregiver does not occur overnight. It takes time, patience, and compassion when working with survivors of childhood sexual abuse.

Similar to a fictional character's journey toward becoming a hero, as a caregiver, you may have (or will) experience a number of trials along your journey toward helping survivors recover from their childhood sexual abuse and navigate recovery through the stages of the healing process. As a professional caregiver, you may know the stages of the healing process for survivors of childhood sexual assault. However, as a loved one to a survivor, you may not know what it means to journey down the path of healing.

Part Two explains the healing process, using Wonder Woman's relationships with Dr. Barbara Ann Minerva (the villain Cheetah) discussed in "Part One: Birth of Your Wonder Woman," Moon Robinson (the villain Mayfly), and Vanessa Kapatelis (the villain Silver Swan) to help explain how battle scars have the potential to develop when attempting to help others heal from past trauma. This portion of the guide outlines trials you may encounter when helping survivors navigate the *healing process*, understanding *complex post-traumatic stress disorder* (C-PTSD), and comprehending the negative thoughts created by *cognitive distortions*. This portion of the book also uses the relationship of Superman and Wonder Woman during the DC Comics event, *The New 52*, to help spouses, partners, and love ones of male survivors understand some of the differences between male and female survivors that may arise when helping males heal from their childhood sexual abuse.

Chapter Four
Mayfly, Wonder Woman, and the Healing Process

"There is no love so great that it cannot be stripped away, leaving you bare before your enemies."

—**Wonder Woman**, *Wonder Woman #79*, "Love's End" (2019)

When attempting to understand the effects of the trauma of childhood sexual abuse, it is important to know that there is no definitive beginning, middle, or end to the healing process. However, there are identifiable landmarks that can assist in navigating the path toward recovery. Research has revealed thirteen steps in the healing process of childhood sexual abuse. Ellen Bass and Laura Davis outline these thirteen steps in *The Courage to Heal* as:

1. The decision to heal
2. The emergency stage
3. Remembering
4. Believing it happened
5. Breaking the silence
6. Understanding it wasn't your fault
7. The child within
8. Grieving
9. Anger
10. Disclosures and truth-telling
11. Forgiveness
12. Spirituality
13. Resolution and moving on

Some survivors never experience two of the previous mentioned steps of the healing process: forgiveness and spirituality. This is because healing from the trauma of sexual abuse does not require forgiving the abuser. Forgiveness for those who have hurt the survivor is linked to religious beliefs, not the process of integrating the memory of being sexually abused. This disconnect between recovery and religion is why some survivors never experience the stage of spirituality in the healing process.

Moving throughout the thirteen stages of recovery takes time and requires that each step be continuously revisited at different times in the survivor's journey of recovery with different insights about themselves, the life they live, and the abuse suffered. Healing cannot take place overnight and cannot be approached as a task in need of being accomplished. Instead, the body and mind progress toward healing at their own pace. It is also important to understand that the healing process is unique for every survivor. This is because no two individuals are the same, and so no two sexual assaults are the same either.

Over the course of this journey toward recovery, life does not come to a stop for the survivor, because healing does not take place in a vacuum. Jobs must be maintained, children must be parented, and other responsibilities must be met. A survivor's responsibilities can create setbacks, relapses, and a need to revisit stages of the healing process that were believed to have already been overcome.

Because healing from child sexual abuse is an extremely personal journey, the healing process of the person you love will be different from another survivor's journey. However, as the author of this guide and a male survivor, I can add some insight into the healing process in an attempt to let you know what to expect while progressing forward.

As stated previously, there are thirteen steps researchers have found that survivors of childhood sexual abuse go through on their journey toward healing. However, as a male survivor who has been actively participating in this process with the help of a therapist, psychiatrist, and medication for over seven years, I discovered that many of the steps I experienced occurred simultaneously rather than separately. The reason for mentioning this is because you may find that the journey of the survivor you care for may be similar.

Many who are beginning to understand recovery view the healing process as a highway with thirteen separate cities along the way that represent the thirteen steps of healing. In the minds of many, there is a large span of miles between each city where life happens. When a city/step is reached, they believe all that is required is filling up with gas, getting food, and stopping to see the sights before moving on to the next destination, eventually reaching their new home at the end of a long drive. Rather, the process is more like a river. This river is large and peaceful at times, slim and rough at others. It contains rapids and lulls and branches into many different smaller streams that flow back into one another. Sometimes, these smaller streams can lead out into open ocean, complicating and confusing the journey, causing the voyager to get lost, revisiting locations multiple times before returning to the correct path to make their way to their new home.

However, rather than thirteen separate steps of the healing process, some stages of the healing process can be combined. To allow exploration of the nature of your abuse with the help of a counselor or therapist trained in childhood sexual abuse, the thirteen steps can be narrowed down to seven stages:

1. The Emergency Stage and the Decision to Heal

2. Remembering and Believing It Happened

3. Grieving and Anger

4. Understanding It Was Not Your Fault and Forgiveness

5. The Child Within

6. Disclosures, Truth-Telling, and Breaking the Silence

7. Spirituality, Forgiveness, and Post-Traumatic Growth

As stated previously, the healing process has no definitive beginning, middle, or end. Although this is true, the emergency stage is usually the most traumatic, determining whether or not the survivor will continue along the road of recovery. Understanding the anxiety and depression that come with triggered memories of the childhood sexual abuse can be difficult, but Wonder Woman and her relationship with Mayfly in *Wonder Woman #51*, "The Fifty-Second Visit" (2018), can help to illustrate the complexity of the healing process, and the needed for patience when helping survivors heal as a caregiver.

Mayfly and Understanding Complex Post-Traumatic Stress Disorder (C-PTSD)

Wonder Woman #51, "The Fifty-Second Visit" (2018), begins with a flashback to a battle between Wonder Woman and Mayfly in *Wonder Woman #28*. Then, Wonder Woman bested the super strong female speedster, putting her behind bars in a maximum-security prison that dampens the superpowers of villains, ensuring she no longer is able to harm another innocent person. "The Fifty-Second Visit" continues the story of Wonder Woman and Mayfly when Diana visits Moon Robinson in prison and attempts to help heal the incarcerated villain when she says, "You are in pain, Moon. I hear it in your words . . . and give you mine. I do not abandon those in pain."

Diana's words may ring true for you as a professional caregiver or loved one of a survivor. You may make similar observations that a survivor is hurting. Similar to the way Diana can hear the pain of Moon Robinson, you may hear the pain in the words or actions of a survivor. Although you may be able to acknowledge the survivor is in pain, they may not be able to notice this pain in themselves, making childhood sexual abuse survivors as resistant to help as Moon when admitting to Diana and herself the amount of pain she was in.

Rather than acknowledge her sadness when Diana tells Moon that she can hear the pain in her words, Moon laughs at the Amazon princess behind the glass of her prison cell and says, "The Amazing Amazon's going to try to figure me out? You're a goddess from an island of immortal women. You've got epithets. How could you understand a damn thing about me?"

Moon goes on to explain her traumatic childhood and her life as a hemophiliac. She explains to Wonder Woman, "I was a surprise. My parents tried, but they had plans for their lives. Carting a kid around wasn't one of them." The images that accompany Moon's words depicted by artist Laura Braga do an excellent job of contrasting Diana's childhood on Themyscira with Moon's childhood in man's world. While Diana was nurtured and encouraged on Paradise Island by her mother and Amazonian sisters, Moon's childhood was filled with isolation following the death of her parents and her fight for survival.

Moon's reluctance to open up to Diana is a result of her **complex post-traumatic stress disorder (C-PTSD)** and helps to explain why survivors of childhood trauma are also afraid to show vulnerability and intimacy with others. C-PTSD is the result of traumatic pain and stress at an early age. As a result of either repeated traumatic events or extreme trauma as an infant, toddler, or adolescent, treating C-PTSD is more difficult than treating PTSD because of the occurrence of trauma during a person's mental development. Arielle Schwartz explains in *The Complex PTSD Workbook* how C-PTSD can be the result of:

- Childhood relationships with parents or caregivers that are frightening, unpredictable, and/or overwhelming
- Ongoing or repeated experiences of neglect or physical, verbal, or sexual abuse
- Growing up with exposure to domestic violence
- Being raised by a caregiver who has an active addiction or untreated mental illness

- Experiencing abuse at especially vulnerable times of development, such as early childhood or adolescence

- Facing severe social stress such as bullying, disability, or exposure to traumatic events within your community without support by a caregiver who projects and cares for you

- Being discriminated against or feeling disempowered without a caregiver who helps advocate for you or takes responsibility for your needs

She goes on to explain later in the workbook how "a core dilemma of C-PTSD is that your longing for connection conflicts with memories that tell you relationships aren't safe." It is for these reasons that Moon Robinson is averse to connecting with Diana and why the survivor you may be attempting to help heal as a caregiver may be averse to making the decision to heal. Moon's brain, like those of survivors of childhood sexual abuse, is using memories of past relationships that were not safe to create cognitive distortions that pushes others away in an attempt to regain a sense of safety and control.

As a professional caregiver or loved one of a survivor, you may attempt to gain the trust of a childhood sexual abuse survivor in the same manner as Diana when she enters Moon's cell to talk with her during their second visit. Wonder Woman risked her physical health when entering the prison cell of the character who attempted to kill her. However, she did not enter the cell due to arrogance or stupidity. She entered in an attempt to gain Moon's trust. As a caregiver, you may act in the same manner as Diana, showing the first signs of vulnerability in an attempt gain the trust of the survivor you are attempting to help heal. Unfortunately, many survivors react in the same manner as Moon. In *Wonder Woman #51*, Moon attempts to kill Diana using different items in her cell during the third, fourth, fifth, and sixth visit, until the only furniture remaining are two small stools. Most survivors will not try and kill their caregivers in the same manner as Moon, but they do lash out with their words in an attempt to protect themselves by pushing others away and keeping them at a distance.

Moon's actions during these first initial visits is similar to the actions of a survivor during the **Emergency Stage** when the survivor fights the overwhelming emotions brought on by memories of the past that can no longer be repressed. The survivor's battle can be external, impacting the lives of others in negative and sometimes harmful ways; or internal, causing panic attacks and thoughts of self-harm and/or suicide. It is the hope of the caregiver that the survivor is reached and helped to know they are safe, in the same way Diana helped to guide Moon toward making the **Decision to Heal**.

Similar to Moon Robinson, many survivors of childhood sexual abuse feel as though they should not have survived their abuse, or wish that they had not. Due to the C-PTSD caused by their childhood trauma, they have a negative view of themselves, believing they are weak because their most precious possession was stripped away—their body. Similar to Moon, survivors often feel weak, afraid, and unsafe in their own bodies, making it so that they do all they can to prevent these emotions. Moon has felt weak her entire life due to being a hemophiliac and the abandonment of her parents, and she wished Wonder Woman had killed her during battle. Instead, Diana tells her, "I've drawn enough blood to know killing you would've been the weak choice. This, visiting here, is hard."

Diana is right when she tells Moon that choosing to heal and helping someone to heal are both hard choices. Recovering from childhood sexual abuse takes a lot of work, compassion, patience, and the exchange of emotions that eventually develops into a relationship between the caregiver and the survivor. Moon and Diana begin to develop this relationship during Wonder Woman's eighth visit. By visit eighteen, Diana opens up to Moon about her life and feelings while eating lunch in an empty cafeteria in front of a squadron of armed guards. On visit twenty-three, Diana and Moon realize similarities in their pasts, and by visit twenty-four, Moon lets down her guard enough to begin building an honest friendship with the superhero. As time progresses from the twenty-ninth visit to the forty-second, Moon addresses her traumatic past and truly begins to heal. By the fifty-first visit, Moon's recovery has progressed so well that she is allowed to walk freely throughout the prison without the dampening of her super abilities.

During this second-to-last visit, as Diana and Moon walk through the prison library, Wonder Woman is attacked by the villain the Inside-Out Man. Unable to focus her attention on the battle due to the anguish of losing a close friend in an earlier battle, Diana is saved by Moon. Afterward, with Inside-Out Man back in custody, Diana opens up to Moon about her own pain. She tells Moon:

> In all these years throughout your sentence, I have never missed a visit. They've become one of my life's few constants. You are the first I've told about Astarte (Wonder Woman's friend). I was not sure I could. But here, now, I felt I needed to tell you. To share my pain with someone who has overcome so much of her own. You've helped me, Moon.

Although these characters are fictional, Diana's confession to Moon, the sharing of her pain and vulnerability, helps to demonstrate the stages of the healing process and its psychological impact not only on survivors, but caregivers as well. It provides context in understanding how helping survivors heal often requires that caregivers become vulnerable in order to gain a survivor's trust and help them progress through the healing process.

Moon Robinson's story in "The Fifty-Second Visit" is also an excellent model to help describe the time needed for survivors to begin trusting. Unfortunately, there are some survivors who view themselves and their actions as those of a victim similar to the way Moon saw herself as a villain following her childhood trauma. This is due to the development of **cognitive distortions** after suffering years of trauma and chronic stress in order to survive. While Moon Robinson is an excellent example to understand the difficulties of the healing process, there is no better example than Vanessa Kapatelis and her transformation into the villain Silver Swan to understand the impact of cognitive distortions on a survivor's view of themselves and others.

Chapter Five
Silver Swan and Cognitive Distortions

"There is nothing in the universe more foolish than love."

—**Anti-Monitor**, *Justice League #36,* "Justice / Doom War: Part 7" (2020)

The villain Silver Swan first appears in *Wonder Woman #288,* "Swan Song," in 1982. Helen Alexandros makes a deal with Ares, the god of war, to kill Wonder Woman in exchange for being granted the beauty and the power to kill any and all men. Author, Roy Williams explains Helen's origin as a girl looked down upon by others (including her mother) for her homely appearance. To combat the negative view others have of her, and she has of herself, Helen performs ballet with the goal of one day dancing the lead in "Swan Lake." Unfortunately, because of her appearance, she is viewed by the producers of her professional traveling ballet troupe as being a good dancer but too ugly to play the lead. Angry and heartbroken, Helen stands on stage and screams to the skies, "Why, you Gods in your far-off heavens? Why did you make me so plain in a world that values beauty over everything?"

Ares hears Helen's pleas and grants her beauty, super strength, flight, and the destructive power of a supersonic scream in exchange for the death of Wonder Woman. In this version of Silver Swan, the villain is allowed her powers for only one hour before transforming back into homely Helen. Helen agrees to the terms of the agreement in hopes of fulfilling Ares' request to destroy Wonder Woman and retain her superpowers permanently, gaining the ability to bring destruction to the world of men.

In 2017, Silver Swan returns to *Wonder Woman,* but reimagined. This time, Silver Swan is Vanessa Kapatelis, an average teenager who loses the use of her legs when rubble falls from a nearby building during a battle between Wonder Woman and a super villain. In the reimagined Silver Swan, Vanessa does not grow bitter due to society's false standards of beauty. Instead, she begins to resent and eventually hate others and herself when she believes Wonder Woman has abandoned her as a friend. Unlike Helen Alexandros, Vanessa is not granted the ability to transform into Silver Swan by the Greek god of war, Ares. Instead, she transforms into the Silver Swan as a result of her own negative thoughts following the injection of nanites into her spine in an attempt to heal her broken legs.

Helen Alexandros and Vanessa Kapatelis both have differences that set the Silver Swan of the past apart from the Silver Swan of the present. However, both are similar in the fact that they transform into the villain Silver Swan as a result of negative thoughts of themselves and others. Using Wonder Woman, Vanessa Kapatelis, and the reimagined villain Silver Swan, this chapter explains how the cognitive distortions of survivors can have adverse effects on their feelings and actions due to the trauma of childhood sexual abuse.

C-PTSD and Cognitive Distortions

As a loved one of a survivor of childhood sexual abuse, you may be confused as to why a survivor's ability to know what should be done to heal sometimes is in contrast to their emotions and actions. This is because of a survivor's development of *cognitive distortions,* negative automatic thoughts caused by C-PTSD that lead a survivor to false assumptions and beliefs about themselves and others as a result of their childhood trauma. **Cognitive Behavior Therapy (CBT),** a form of therapy developed by Dr. Aaron Beck, identifies cognitive distortions in an attempt to help survivors change negative automatic thoughts into true statements free of any distortion. When helping survivors, there are usually ten common cognitive distortions that are identified in CBT as affecting survivors of childhood sexual abuse.

1. **All-or-Nothing Thinking:** Things are viewed in absolute black-and-white categories. This means there can only be a right and a wrong answer, with no gray areas in between. These thoughts lead some survivors to view themselves as being either a hero or a villain. To grow and heal, survivors must move beyond all-or-nothing thinking and examine situations completely to understand the full effects of their thoughts.

2. **Overgeneralizations:** A negative event is viewed as a never-ending pattern of defeat. This means that survivors view actions and themselves through the lens of a victim rather than a survivor. The survivor believes the world is always against them and there is no way to win. So, why try? This sense of isolation and defeatism only leads to shame because the survivor could not prevent the sexual abuse.

3. **Mental Filters:** The survivor dwells on negatives rather than positives. Some thoughts during this cognitive distortion may be: "What's the point?", "Even if I try I'll still fail," or "It's better to not get my hopes up so I won't be disappointed later." Viewing only the negative will lead to negative thoughts of themselves as the cause of their downfall, rather than their rise and eventual success.

4. **Discounting the Positives:** The survivor insists that their accomplishments or positive qualities don't count. This means that the survivor never views the positive in their actions. Rather, the good things are because of the actions of others. This distortion ensures they always view themselves as the villain, unable to win, and providing a small amount of power in believing they can control their own fate.

5. **Jumping to Conclusions:**

   a. **Mind Reading:** The survivor assumes others are acting negatively without definite evidence. Some common thoughts may be: "Because of the way they said it, I knew they were mad at me," or "I could tell by the way they were standing they were annoyed," or "It's not what they said, but what they didn't say." While mind reading may have been useful as a child to anticipate when future abuses would take place, as an adult it only provides wasted energy to not feel ashamed or at fault for the sexual abuse.

   b. **Fortune-Telling:** The survivor arbitrarily believes circumstances will turn out badly. Without justification or warrant, they assume the worse. This is done to limit their amount of hope, because as a child, hope was a luxury that could not be afforded if it meant surviving. Fortune-telling allows survivors to anticipate the worst and remain hypervigilant in protecting themselves from the chaos and loss of control that was a product of their sexual abuse.

6. **Magnification or Minimization:** The survivor blows situations out of proportion or shrinks their importance. This means placing value in the wrong place. While the emotions of a survivor may be minimized, the importance of others may be inflated, in some instances allowing them to remain unnoticed and protected through invisibility. In other circumstances, it means continuing to identify as the victim to create chaos in the lives of others to maintain a sense of control.

7. **Emotional Reasoning:** The survivor reasons with how they feel. This means believing that if they feel a certain way, then that must be what they are. For example, the survivor may say to themselves, "I feel worthless, so I must be worthless." This distortion allows continued feelings of doubt and worthlessness, while allowing a limited sense of control through false prophecies destined to come true.

8. **"Should" or "Shouldn't Have" Statements:** The survivor criticizes themselves and their actions through "should," "ought to," "must," and "have to." This distortion puts unwarranted stress on the survivor in belief of what they must have or shouldn't have done. It allows the survivor to abuse themselves verbally, saying things in their mind that they would never say to their worst enemy, while reaffirming the beliefs of their abuser that they are worthless, and the abuse was their fault.

9. **Labeling:** Instead of stating, "I made a mistake," the survivor calls themselves names such as "stupid" or "idiot." Stating these words dehumanizes their actions and helps to reaffirm the way the abuser made them feel during and following the sexual abuse. These thoughts force the survivor to view themselves as less and the abuse as being their own doing.

10. **Personalization and Blame:** The survivor blames themselves for something they were not entirely responsible for, or they blame others while denying their role in the problem. In either circumstance, it means playing the victim. It ensures a semblance of control through a false belief of control and accountability that was never their own, or righteousness in the false belief that they are completely innocent of all wrongdoing because of the sexual abuse endured in the past resulting in the victimization of the present.

To better understanding the effects of these ten cognitive distortions on the thoughts, feelings, and actions of a survivor, there is no better character than Vanessa Kapatelis and her transformation into the Silver Swan.

Swan Song

Wonder Woman #38-40 (2017) tells the story of Vanessa Kapatelis and her transformation into Silver Swan. Told from the first-person point of view of Vanessa, the teenager explains how rubble from a battle with Wonder Woman and Major Disaster fell from a nearby building, crushing her legs. Although the accident prevented Vanessa from walking, it did allow the teenager to begin developing a friendship with Wonder Woman. Concerned for Vanessa's well-being, the superhero visited the hospital to check on the teenager's recovery following an experimental procedure using nanites to help heal Vanessa's legs. Vanessa explains the beginning of her relationship with Wonder Woman on the first few pages of *Wonder Woman #38* when she states:

> *My mom said she was proud of how brave I was being, but it wasn't hard when I had Wonder Woman there to inspire me. I'll never forget when she told me to call her Diana. She visited me often—nothing fancy, we'd just sit and talk . . . I have to be strong and look ahead, like Diana would. So, here I am, happy more often than I'm sad. My name is Vanessa Kapatelis, and I'm Wonder Woman's best friend.*

Unfortunately, Vanessa's positive outlook on life does not last. Over time, the busy life of a superhero causes Diana to stop visiting. Later, Vanessa feels further abandoned by the people she loves when her mother is killed during a freak car crash. Sitting alone on her hospital bed, Vanessa thinks of the loss of her legs, the death of her mother, the abandonment by Diana, and says to herself, "I'm angry. I'm hurt. I've lost my mother, and it feels like I've lost Diana too. My name is Vanessa Kapatelis, and I'm no one's best friend."

Time moves forward, and Vanessa begins to view herself more and more as a victim. The young girl finally transforms into a villain when witnessing Wonder Woman save a husband, wife, and their newborn baby following an attack by a super-villain. Devastated and broken, Vanessa says to herself, "There! A family she just saved—like with me—during a fight with a super-villain. But unlike me, they're all still on their feet. Unlike me, they aren't alone. Unlike me, they're Diana's friends now."

Soon afterward, Vanessa's negative thoughts trigger the nanites in her body to transform her into Silver Swan, a villain with metallic wings and razor-sharp claws. Seeking revenge for the abandonment of Diana, Silver Swan kills the Darling family Wonder Woman saved on the news, and says, "My name is Vanessa Kap— No! My name is Silver Swan, and I'm Wonder Woman's worst enemy."

Although, Vanessa Kapatelis is a fictional character of the DC universe, her thoughts are not unique to her alone. Similar to the thoughts of survivors who have yet to make the decision to heal, Vanessa's thoughts following the loss of her legs and death of her mother are filled with cognitive distortions that eventually cause her to transform into a villain, Silver Swan. By analyzing Vanessa's cognitive distortions, it may help you as a caregiver recognize the cognitive distortions of the survivor you may be seeking to help heal.

The Cognitive Distortions of Silver Swan

Vanessa suffers from many of the above-mentioned cognitive distortions before and while being the villain Silver Swan. Below, Vanessa's negative automatic thoughts from *Wonder Woman #38-40* are examined and explained in an attempt to help you as a professional caregiver or loved one of a survivor understand how to identify when and if a survivor is exhibiting a cognitive distortion.

All-or-Nothing Thinking

As stated above, all-or-nothing thinking is when a survivor views circumstances in black-and-white categories rather than allowing any room for alternate thoughts. Vanessa Kapatelis demonstrates all-or-nothing thinking multiple times throughout the three-part *Wonder Woman* "Swan's Song." Each time Vanessa expresses this cognitive distortion, she reinforces the polarizing black-and-white belief often demonstrated by survivors.

The first time she exhibits this cognitive distortion is when she states, "My name is Vanessa Kapatelis, and I'm Wonder Woman's best friend." Here, Vanessa's words reinforce Vanessa's belief that she has to have it all by being Wonder Woman's best friend or nothing at all. For her, there is no middle ground. Vanessa must be Wonder Woman's best friend or her enemy. Her contrasting thoughts reinforce this cognitive distortion while sitting alone in her hospital bed. She says to her herself, "My names is Vanessa Kapatelis, and I'm no one's best friend." Vanessa views herself as either being Wonder Woman's best friend or viewing the heroine as a villain in need of being destroyed.

Similar to Vanessa, survivors often demonstrate a similar form of black-and-white thinking that leads to viewing themselves and others as villains. Allowing contrasting thoughts that exist in the grey area between the black-and-white makes survivors feel less safe due to being less in control. Your goal as a caregiver is the same as Wonder Woman attempting to help Vanessa change her thoughts in order to see the truth in her negative actions as Silver Swan. Rather than fight villains with silver bracelets and a golden lasso, as a caregiver you help survivors using cognitive behavior therapy to identify, battle, and transform their negative, automatic, all-or-nothing thoughts in order to feel safe being less hypervigilant in their actions.

Overgeneralization

As stated previously, overgeneralization is when a survivor views a negative event as a never-ending cycle of defeat. Vanessa begins to overgeneralize the truth of her reality, viewing her life as a never-ending cycle of tragedies, beginning with the loss of her legs and ending with the death of her mother.

Vanessa begins overgeneralizing when she says to herself, "All I know is the shock of Mom's passing affected me. I can't walk again. Square one." The negative automatic thoughts later continue when she says to herself, "I'm angry. I'm hurt. I've lost my mother, and it feels like I've lost Diana too."

Vanessa overgeneralizes to the point of transforming into Silver Swan after watching Wonder Woman rescue and reunite an infant with the Darlings. While watching the television screen, she says, "But unlike me, they're all still on their feet. Unlike me, they aren't alone. Unlike me, they're Diana's friends now."

Vanessa views the tragedies in her life as a perpetuating cycle of traumatic events out of her sphere of control. This lack of control leads to resentment and anger at seeing the happiness of others. Similar to Vanessa, a survivor's cognitive distortion of overgeneralization leads to viewing the negatives in their life rather than the positives. As a caregiver, you can help survivors battle overgeneralization by helping them see that sometimes in life bad things, such as natural disasters, pandemics, and even sexual abuse, happen to good people. These horrific events are outside the sphere of an individual's control and do not make the survivor weak or evil. There is nothing they could have done, said, or worn to prevent their trauma from occurring. As humans, life is filled with both beauty and horrors beyond control. Although this is true, survivors have the opportunity to regain some of the power that was taken from them by learning to understand and take control of their negative automatic thoughts.

Mental Filters

When a survivor begins to mentally filter their thoughts, they only focus on the negatives of a given situation rather than the positives. In *Wonder Woman #40*, "Swan's Song: Conclusion" (2018), Vanessa Kapatelis fully transforms into the villain Silver Swan when she begins mentally filtering her thoughts to only view the negatives in a situation.

Vanessa seeks revenge against Wonder Woman, believing the heroine abandoned her in her time of need, by killing an innocent family and attempting to kill Diana's brother, Jason. Filled with rage, Silver Swan says to herself while flying in the night sky, "Vanessa was weak. She looked up to Wonder Woman. She thought her a friend. I am not Vanessa, and the moon reflects the cold silver of my dead heart."

Silver Swan's words are an example of what it means to exhibit the cognitive distortion of a mental filter. Rather than see the good in herself, Silver Swan views her actions when she was Vanessa as weak. The villain sees herself in this manner because of her feelings of fear after losing the use of her legs and the death of her mother. The mental filter of viewing herself as weak provides Vanessa with a sense of control, safety, and strength in knowing there is no reason to try, because failure will always be the outcome.

Survivors of childhood sexual abuse use similar mental filters to provide themselves with a sense of control, safety, and restoration of power following their fear filled and chaotic past. As a caregiver, helping survivors to use cognitive behavior therapy strategies have the potential to provide an opportunity to heal from their traumatic past rather than cope using ineffective tools that eventually cause more harm than good.

Personalization and Blame

As stated previously, personalization and blame occurs when a survivor either personalizes a negative event, blaming themselves, or they push all the blame of negative events in their life on others. In "Swan Song," Vanessa both personalizes and blames others for her negative actions.

Vanessa suffers from the cognitive distortion of blaming Wonder Woman when she murders the Darling family as Silver Swan. While battling Silver Swan, Diana attempts to make sense of Vanessa's transformation by examining how the nanites are physically and mentally altering her friend. Rather than accept Diana's explanation, Vanessa deflects blame away from herself and back onto Wonder Woman when she says, "Is that what you think? That's the grand pronouncement of the almighty warrior? Nothing's wrong with my mind. I'm angry with you, but that doesn't mean I'm crazy."

Blame can also be seen in Vanessa's words during battle with Diana in *Wonder Woman #750*, "Always" (2020), when she says to

Wonder Woman, "You didn't save me that day you pulled me out from under rubble. You just wanted to look like a hero for the cameras. But as soon as the adoring crowd stopped watching, you abandoned me, and now you have to deal with the consequences."

As a caregiver, your job is to try and help survivors understand the message behind Diana's words when she tells Vanessa, "You blame me for what you've become, but you're wrong. You are the only person who can decide your actions." Understanding and accepting that each individual is responsible for their own actions (whether good or bad) is the key difference between identifying as a victim or making the decision to heal as a survivor.

Although Vanessa blames Wonder Woman for her actions as Silver Swan, she also personalizes her feelings of being weak and stupid, as she puts it, for trusting Wonder Woman. Viewing her actions in this negative manner allows Vanessa to believe there is nothing she could have done to save herself from the tragedies she has encountered in her life. Silver Swan's words also allow Vanessa to justify her actions as a character who is only attempting to keep herself safe, not to intentionally do harm to others. Survivors are often subject to similar cognitive distortions when viewing and calling themselves "weak" and "stupid." These thoughts provide them with a false sense of safety in believing there is nothing they can do to save themselves from the pain of their traumatic past. This places the fault of the abuse on themselves rather than holding their abuser accountable for their actions.

Healing

As a professional caregiver or ally of a survivor of childhood sexual abuse, cognitive distortions can make healing difficult. The negative automatic thoughts survivors exhibit as cognitive distortions may have been learned, repeated, and reinforced due to years of victimization. This means that transforming negative automatic thoughts into true statements free of cognitive distortion takes repeated practice, guidance, and positive support. The guides

Heroes, Villains, and Healing and *How to Master Your Inner Superman* provide survivors with writing exercises to help identify and transform their child and parental thoughts into the true statements of an adult. A professional caregiver or ally provides support and compassion for the survivor as they progress down their journey of healing in the same way Diana provides support to Vanessa when helping her reconcile with her past actions as Silver Swan.

In *Wonder Woman #750,* "Always" (2020), the nanites are extracted from Vanessa Kapatelis's body, preventing her from transforming into Silver Swan. Alone in the ARGUS Inpatient Recovery Facility, Vanessa wrestles with her past actions. She says to herself, "My name is Vanessa Kapatelis, and I never thought I was a bad person. I always ate my peas, always listened to my mother, always recycled and used turn signals. I thought when the going got tough, I could handle it with grace. And I did until I broke."

Throughout the comic, she recounts her relationship with Wonder Woman, her transformation into Silver Swan, and the innocent lives she took while seeking to harm the hero she called her friend. In the end, she believes she deserves to be alone and that she does not deserve to heal. It is at that moment Diana walks through the door, proving to Vanessa and the reader that although the teenager should be held accountable for her actions, everyone deserves to heal from their past trauma. She tells Vanessa, "I believe in you. I know we can get through this. If you need me, I will be there. Always."

In that moment, Diana does the same thing for Vanessa that you do for survivors as a caregiver. You and Wonder Woman provide hope, support, and reinforce the belief that everyone deserves to heal no matter what may have been done in the past when attempting to cope with the trauma of childhood sexual abuse. As humans, we all make mistakes. It is for this reason we all deserve to be forgiven and to forgive ourselves.

Chapter Six
Helping Male Survivors Heal from Childhood Sexual Abuse

"But we chose you because above everything you're a man of empathy. And empathy isn't about ideals. It's about sharing our weaknesses, too. Our fears."

—**Superman**, *Justice League #7*, "The Totality: Conclusion" (2018)

Author George Perez made *Wonder Woman* (in my opinion) into the powerhouse comic book it is today. Using a fantastic blend of Greek mythology, traditional characters from the forties, new heroes and old villains that help and hinder the heroine in her battle against evil, and the gritty artistry of the eighties make *Wonder Woman #1-7*, "Gods and Mortals" (1987), a comic that pushes readers to the edge of their seat.

What makes *Wonder Woman #1* so compelling then and now is Perez's ability to discuss universal themes of good, evil, love, and humanity in a way that can be easily understood regardless of the somewhat absurdity of the content. The first two pages of "Gods and Mortals" are a testament to this. Although the setting of the comic is over thirty thousand years in the past, Perez provides readers with a modern understanding of trauma and gender norms using prehistoric man, woman, and murder. The comic also provides an understanding of how trauma affects the way many male survivors view their childhood sexual abuse, providing an explanation for why they may interact negatively with caregivers seeking to help them heal.

The comic begins with a man dressed in an animal loin cloth leaning against the entrance of a cave and nursing a missing hand. A pregnant woman exits the cave to try and relieve the man's pain. George Perez narrates the story alongside images of torment. He writes:

> *30,000 BC—Today, your tribe cast you out! They mocked you, called you useless. Called you an animal! Only yesterday you were called a man! You hunted with men and the sabretooth. The one who bested you. The one who took your hand! Now, you are a man no more. For men are hunters, and hunters need hands! That makes you afraid, but you must not show your fear. Remember what the tribe teaches. Fear is for women! So, you hide your face, quell your trembling. Still, somehow, she knows! And when she touches you. When you hear her sympathetic whining. You curse her! So, you pull away, but she insists! You try to ignore her, but her whimpering taunts you. Teases you. Emasculates you. Makes you . . . snap! And when your temper cools. When the echo of her scream has been swallowed by the air. You hear it! A muffled stirring within her. And a voice, as if from the Earth itself, whispering, calling, beckoning, making something happen that you cannot understand! And it makes you want to scream!*

These words describe the actions of a fictional man from 30,000 BC, but they ring true when describing the thoughts, actions, and feelings of modern male survivors when confronting traumatic memories of childhood sexual abuse.

Male survivors of childhood sexual abuse have not suffered the trauma of losing a hand while battling a sabretooth tiger. However, similar to the prehistoric man in the comic, modern men also suppress feelings of fear, making them feel weak, helpless, unable to fulfill the perpetrated definition of what it means to be a "real man."

In "Gods and Mortals," the prehistoric man does not see how he can ever be a real man, and be accepted by his tribe of real men, if he cannot hunt. Similarly, male survivors do not see how they can ever be real men if they have been sexually abused. This is because male survivors believe sexual abuse and assault only happens to females and that real men should always want and initiate sex.

Both the prehistoric man in "Gods and Mortals" and many male survivors view emotions as a sign of weakness, worthy only for the lesser tribe of women. It is for this reason that when offered help, many male survivors grow angry, resist healing, and lash out at those they love. Both versions of men hurt the person they care for, viewing themselves and their actions as those of a villain.

When helping male survivors, it is important to know why they may resist healing from their childhood trauma so vehemently— Why they may hurt those they care for with their words and actions, and why they may take the pain of their abuse out on themselves in the form of self-harm, addiction, and suicide. Knowing why is the best way to help guide male survivors down the path of recovery.

The Boy Code and Becoming a Real Man

Boys are socialized from a young age to follow the **boy code**, described by William S. Pollack, associate clinical professor of psychology at Harvard Medical School, and author of *Real Boys: Rescuing Our Sons from the Myths of Boyhood*, as needing to follow the false truths of:

- **The sturdy oak:** Men should be stoic, independent, and refrain from showing weakness.

- **Give 'em hell:** Boys and men should be macho, take risks, and use violence.

- **The big wheel:** Men should demonstrate their power and dominance and how they've got everything under control, even when they don't.

- **No sissy stuff:** Real men don't cry or display emotions that might be viewed as feminine; doing so leaves men open to being labeled as "sissies" or "fags."

The indoctrination of these stereotypes at such a young age leads men to suffer in silence and self-medicate with drugs and alcohol abuse rather than seek help through counseling or therapy. The boy code perpetuates the belief that boys should learn to hold in their emotions, deal with them personally, and that given enough time they will go away. These beliefs lead to alcohol and other substance-related disorders, sleep disorders, pyromania, intermittent explosive disorder, pathological gambling, and sexual disorders such as exhibitionism, pedophilia, and voyeurism, according to a Prevention Institute study in 2014.

To live by the boy code and survive in hostile environments, male survivors adapt as children to become hypersensitive to the reactions and behaviors of others. Judith Herman explains in *Trauma and Recovery* that:

> Adaptation to this climate of constant danger requires a state of constant alertness. Children in an abusive environment develop extraordinary abilities to scan for warning signs of attack. They become minutely attuned to their abusers' inner states. They learn to recognize subtle changes in facial expressions and body language as signals of anger, sexual arousal, intoxication, or dissociation. This nonverbal communication becomes highly automatic and occurs for the most part outside of conscious awareness.

Survivors of childhood sexual abuse behave with hypersensitivity because their survival depends on it. Without this ability, making an incorrect move as a child could result in physical, psychological, or sexual danger, even the possibility of death. Similar to the prehistoric cave man in *Wonder Woman #1*, "Gods and Mortals," males have the added hinderance of living by the unspoken rules of the boy code in order to be seen by others as the embodiment of being a real man.

Attempting to live by the boy code as a male survivor of childhood sexual abuse creates fear, shame, and feelings of helplessness. When left unaddressed, the fear caused after being sexually abused has the potential to transform into anger, either expressed outward on others or inward on the survivor himself. The fear and anger that is directed inward does not go away. Instead, the effects of the childhood trauma attack the mind and body. This is especially true for male survivors of trauma and can be seen in 2018 research and data from Men's Health Forum in the UK where they find that:

- Just over three out of four suicides (76 percent) are by men.
- Suicide is the biggest cause of death for men under thirty-five.
- Men are nearly three times more likely than women to become alcohol dependent.
- Men are less likely to access psychological therapies than women.
- Only 36 percent of references to increased access to psychological therapies are men.

In the US, the state of men's mental health is no better. According to the American Foundation for Suicide Prevention, men die by suicide 3.54 times more often than women. And according to Mental Health America, one in five adults experiences a mental health problem each year resulting in:

- Over six million men suffering from depression per year.
- Males being less likely than women to seek help for depression, substance abuse, and stressful life events because of social norms, reluctance to talk, and downplaying symptoms.
- One in five men developing alcohol dependency during his life.

- Male suicide being the seventh leading cause of death among males.

These statistics help shed some light on the mental state of men and the long-lasting effects of childhood sexual abuse in the form of C-PTSD on their mental, emotional, and physical health. To cope with this trauma as a child and into adulthood, male survivors develop an ability similar to that of Clark Kent hiding his identity as Superman. It is called *doublethink*. This is when male survivors create a *double-self* in an attempt to remain safe and make sense of their hostile environment.

Double-thinking means having the ability to create and keep positive thoughts and memories, either through the lens of the survivor or the environment of which he is a part, while possessing memories of utter despair alongside those of joy. Survivors develop this coping mechanism in order to preserve the possibility of hope and the chance of a possible savior. As a male survivor, this means knowing they were sexually abused as a child while also knowing (and sometimes even perpetuating the belief) that men and boys cannot be sexually abused or raped. The ability to double-think walls off the abuse to help minimize its effects, rationalize why the abuse occurred, or excuse the abuse altogether, allowing the survivor to function, make sense of their abuse, and remain sane while navigating a hostile environment.

Double-thinking also creates double self-images for the survivor, fragmenting his identity. Male survivors often view themselves and their actions as being tainted or bad. They believe their past abuse gives them the strength to save others. This is because some male survivors believe they are beyond redemption, able to endure what others cannot. These are the thoughts of male survivors who view themselves and their actions as heroes. Other survivors view themselves and their past actions as irredeemable, making them believe they are beyond salvation. These are the male survivors who view themselves and their actions as those of a villain.

Both hero and villain perspectives of male survivors are fragmented and flawed, forcing survivors to view their surroundings through the black-and-white lens of a comic book that cannot be maintained into adulthood. While effective as children, the double-thoughts and double-selves cannot exist together when trying to navigate adult relationships. Soon, possibly in their late twenties or early to mid-thirties, male survivors realize their world is not a comic book, forcing the black-and-white images of superheroes and villains to shatter. The tools once used to survive and make sense of themselves, their actions, others, and their environment become less effective as the denial of their childhood trauma becomes impossible, making the reality that men and boys can be sexually assaulted becomes more apparent.

Male survivors often view themselves as a hero always capable of helping others. They consider themselves mentally, emotionally, and physically stable enough to handle anything life throws their way. However, what happens when male survivors enter the Emergency Stage of the healing process? They no longer view themselves as a strong and confident savior of others. Instead, they feel weak and afraid as memories of past abuse trigger crippling panic attacks.

As a caregiver, how do you help these male survivors who have lived by the boy code most of their lives and are resistant to healing? There is no better example to help understand how to help guide male survivors down the path of recovery than analyzing the intimate relationship of Wonder Woman and Superman during the DC Comics event, *The New 52.*

The Intimate Relationship of Superman and Wonder Woman

To say that Superman's timeline throughout the DC universe is confusing would be an understatement. The Man of Steel has died, come back to life, and altered his origin too many times to count. Although it is common knowledge that Superman is Clark Kent, and Clark Kent is head over heels in love with Lois Lane, there is a time during *The New 52* when Superman and Wonder Woman are a superpowered couple.

In *The New 52*, the timelines of classic characters such as Batman, Superman, and Wonder Woman are slightly altered due to the mishaps of the superhero Flash in the graphic novel *Flashpoint*. In this alternate timeline, Superman and Wonder Woman fall in love. As with any relationship, there are highs when the lovers can't live without one another, lows when the person you love transforms into the villain, and doomsdays making you believe the only way to move forward is to wipe them from the face of existence. This is especially true of Superman and Wonder Woman as they attempt to create a life together while being continuously forced to put their relationship on hold as they race off to save the world. Both superheroes love one another, but as time progresses they no longer see eye to eye, growing further and further apart until the relationship fizzles into nonexistence.

The relationship and eventual separation of the Big Blue Boy Scout and the Amazon princess offer a model for what it needed when helping male survivors heal from their childhood sexual abuse. The comics used as examples take place when Clark loses his powers as Superman, leaving him vulnerable and no longer able to see himself as a superhero. Feeling weak and helpless, he no longer views himself as compatible with Wonder Woman.

<u>Vulnerability</u>

In 2017's *Superman/Wonder Woman Volume 5*, "A Savage End," there is a period of twenty-four hours when Superman has lost his superpowers. While in a particularly difficult battle, Superman expels all of the solar energy stored in his cells in one high-powered solar flare. The Man of Steel's new super ability was useful in defeating the Galactic Golem but leaves him vulnerable for a day as his cells recharge.

During this period, Clark decides to take advantage of his temporary humanity to cook dinner and spend some distraction free time with his girlfriend, Diana Prince. Unfortunately, Diana is called away to battle as Wonder Woman before the two can sit down to eat the romantic candle-lit dinner prepared by Clark. Rather than let the superpowered woman he loves go fight evil alone, Clark insists that he can help as Superman even without his abilities. Wonder Woman does not agree, viewing Clark as more of a liability when battling a demonic tentacled monster with razor-sharp teeth. Rather than argue, Wonder Woman leaves to battle the monster as Clark sits in his apartment alone, stewing over the loss of his powers and his feelings of uselessness.

When Wonder Woman returns from battle, an argument between the two lovers ensues. Clark believes he could have helped, telling Diana, "I'm not helpless! I can still contribute. I can still fight. I am more than just my powers!" Diana explains how she knows he is more than just his superpowers but was attempting to keep him safe. When Clark says he did not ask her to keep him safe, Diana realizes why the hero is truly upset. She tells Clark, "You said it yourself. There's always some emergency, someone who needs saving. You're always the one helping everyone else. It's who you are. So that doesn't make it easy to be on the other side, does it? To sit it out, and let someone protect you."

Wonder Woman's words hit home when explaining why many male survivors who view themselves as Superman may be reluctant to show vulnerability. As a man attempting to live by the rules of the boy code, male survivors believe they are the ones who must always save the day. Unfortunately, when healing, male survivors must rely on others for strength, protection, and a sense of safety. As a result of living by the boy code, these are skills that may have never been encouraged to develop. Throughout most of the lives of male survivors, showing vulnerability may have been seen as a weakness that was never nurtured to grow due to societal standards of what it means to be a real man.

This belief of not being able to show vulnerability because of an attempt to try and appear in control is not only true for male survivors, but professional caregivers as well. As a therapist, counselor, or first responder, showing vulnerability may be perceived as a weakness by other caregivers, administrators, or even yourself. Asking for support when helping others heal from their traumatic past may be viewed as a sign by some that you as a caregiver "can't take the heat" if you lean on others during times when feeling weak and vulnerable and support is needed to save your inner Wonder Woman.

Superman, Wonder Woman, and Failing Forward

Occasionally, there is a problem with loved ones attempting to protect male survivors from harm rather than allowing them to feel emotions that may be painful but necessary to grow and heal. Unfortunately, this is sometimes viewed as an encroachment on a male survivor's ability to feel strong and capable as a man. In these circumstances, although caregivers believe they are attempting to keep the person they love safe, their actions are not always beneficial to helping the survivor heal. Instead, their actions are counterproductive, preventing the survivor from feeling the full spectrum of emotions. Pain, sadness, and anger are emotions that have been negatively stigmatized by societal standards, but they are necessary for survivors to experience alongside joy, tranquility, and relief when making the choice to journey down the path of recovery. As a caregiver, empathy and support is needed to help survivors heal. However, allowing survivors to experience both positive and negative emotions when remembering the trauma of their abuse is the difference between helping survivors to heal and attempting to save the survivors from recovering.

Wonder Woman makes this mistake in *Superman/Wonder Woman Volume 4: Dark Truth* (2016). Here, Superman begins to lose his abilities, making him more of a man than a Kryptonian. Diana's view of herself as a protector rather than a supportive lover is evident in the first few lines of the comic. As Clark sleeps, she lies beside him in bed, thinking to herself, "A friendship forged. Our love born. New power realized and others taken away. His secret revealed. So much, so fast. Finding respite where we can. From the tempest of change all around us. I am his sentinel and no harm will come to my love while I draw breath."

These lines set the tone for the rest of the comic when Wonder Woman attempts to protect her weakening lover at all costs. Tensions between the two superhero lovers begin to come to a head when Diana lies to Clark.

In the comic, Superman's secret identity has been discovered by the world. In an attempt to understand how a superpowered alien was able to live in the small town of Smallville, Kansas, without detection, the US government begins kidnapping and interrogating Clark's closest friends and family to discover what they do and do not know about the superhero's secret identity. Concerned, Clark goes to the White House to seek answers from the president. Before doing so, he asks Diana to not interfere. This is because he did not want both of them to be seen by the public as going rogue if he was forced to break the law to get the answers he needed.

Rather than listen, Diana goes behind Clark's back to locate the missing people with Steve Trevor. She is successful, but rather than contact Clark when she discovers the location of the secret government facility holding Clark's friends, she enters the facility alone and uses her lasso of truth to discover what each does and does not know about Superman's history and secret identity as Clark Kent.

When Clark is successful and arrives at the facility to find Wonder Woman using her lasso on the people he cares for, the superhero is not happy. He tells both Lois Lane and Diana before leaving to try and restore his powers, "Look. You both made a distinct choice, and as much as I hate even saying it . . . pure and simple . . . you both betrayed my trust. You want to rationalize it for yourselves, but when all's said and done, that's what you did, so don't expect me to be happy about it or tell you it's okay."

Although Clark expresses his frustrations and desire to not be followed, Diana betrays his trust for the final time.

Clark believes that if he pilots a spacecraft as close as possible to the sun, the radiation will recharge his cells, restoring his powers to their former glory. After knocking out Flash and hijacking a spacecraft, Clark flies toward the sun from the Justice League watchtower in orbit above Earth. When Diana realizes Clark's plan, she goes to the watchtower, wakes up Flash, follows behind in another spacecraft, and tells Flash to teleport both her and Superman back to the watchtower when in range of Superman. Wonder Woman reaches Superman inches from the surface of the sun. As Flash teleports both heroes back to the watchtower, Clark looks into Wonder Woman's eyes and says, "Diana, I don't know if I love you anymore."

The relationship of Superman and Wonder Woman does not come to an end because Diana does not care for Clark, who is clearly hurting. It comes to an end because of a lack of communication and trust between them both.

It is true that Clark was weak and needed help to ensure his safety. However, it is also true that Diana betrayed his trust in an attempt to keep the person she loves from harm. Both heroes were at fault, which helps to illustrate that helping the person you care for heal from the trauma of childhood sexual abuse requires communication that can only be accomplished if there is trust. Without trust, C-PTSD will not allow the survivor to build the relationship needed to combat the adverse childhood experiences of their past. The key to succeeding in helping guide a male survivor toward making the decision to heal is communication, helping them to succeed, allowing them to fail, letting the survivor know you are strong enough to shoulder some of their burden but also worth sharing a life together. This means being open to communicating when one should lead and the other should follow. Neither demonstrates weakness. It shows strength in knowing when help is needed.

This is not easy, and it cannot be accomplished alone. Couples therapy and counseling should always be an option to remain open with the other about what is and is not being fulfilled in the relationship. A trained professional can provide both the survivor and the partner with the tools needed to succeed. The other guides, *Heroes, Villains, and Healing, How to Kill Your Batman,* and *How to Master Your Inner Superman,* are also great resources that provide writing exercises that help the healing process while identifying learned coping mechanisms using other DC Comic heroes and villains.

It is helpful for male survivors to know that they are not alone and you will be there to help, using the strength, compassion, and love of Wonder Woman, while also helping him know that he does not have to be Superman. He can be vulnerable. He can hurt. It is the only way to truly heal.

Final Note

It is important to note that some relationships are unable to be saved. This is a difficult fact to accept as truth for numerous reasons and innumerable circumstances, but just because a person was hurt in the past, it does not give them the right to hurt others. No one can tell you as a loved one of a survivor if your relationship can be saved. However, if one person's healing is at the expense of another's physical, emotional, or mental health, the relationship should be reassessed to ensure everyone is safe. It is true that healing cannot be accomplished alone, but the journey may not include you. Although you may wish to help the survivor you love, professional help from a licensed counselor, therapist, or psychiatrist can help the healing process of the survivor in ways you may not be able to notice.

Seeking help from a professional to discuss anxiety and stress applies to you as a caregiver as well. Although you may not have suffered childhood sexual abuse, helping a survivor heal can cause feelings of burnout, compassion fatigue, and secondary traumatic stress of your own. The following chapters discuss how to recognize and battle these overwhelming emotions in order to practice trauma stewardship and save your inner Wonder Woman.

Chapter Seven
The Black Boy Code
(Autobiographical)

"An age without love is an age of villains."

—**Veronica Cale**, *Wonder Woman # 79,* "Loveless: Part 3" (2019)

What it means to fulfill the definition of being a "real man" is different for each male. It is true that the boy code guides the actions of boys throughout adolescence and into adulthood, but the boy code is also different for different cultures and ethnicities. As a caregiver, it is important to know that these differences do exist and make healing from childhood sexual abuse more difficult to understand. Although my wife, Sarah, and I were best friends for three years, dated for one year, and were engaged for another before getting married, she is still learning about the effects of the black boy code on the way I view others, myself, healing, family, and relationships. It took a long time to understand my black boy code while coming of age in Peoria, Illinois, during the nineties.

The following excerpt is from *Raped Black Male: A Memoir*. It is a somewhat humorous interpretation of my black boy code and how it shaped my view of manhood. As a caregiver, it is important to keep in mind that the boy code for some males is more complex than others due to cultural, race, and class differences that can only be understood with time, trust, patience, and relationship building.

How Black Are You?

The idea of blackness never goes away. The question is always there. Am I black enough? And many times, the answer is no, I'm not, but I am me. Accepting the fact that I love going for a run when I've had a hard day, and that being on the Bowling Green State University Speech and Debate Team comes to mind rather than going to parties, makes me happy. The truth is, I'm a nerd; there's nothing I can do about it, and there's nothing wrong with it. Although, going to therapy has recently made me question that.

You see, when a person is raped at such a young age and has no way of dealing with the pain, it creates a form of post-traumatic stress. When the act occurs, it takes control away from the individual, leaving them feeling helpless, whether they know it or not. It makes them feel as if nothing is under their control; they live in a state of fear. This fear leaves them with two options:

- **Option 1: Give in.** The victim self-medicates in the form of alcohol, cigarettes, drugs, sex, or all of the above. His ability to make rational decisions has been taken along with his sense of control. He is lost and has no way of finding himself. Many of the decisions he makes about his life, job, and relationships seem wrong to others, because they are. Decisions are foreign, and he goes through life making one poor decision after another without truly knowing why, unless he seeks help.

- **Option 2: Control everything.** The victim thinks, and so feels, that because control was taken away from him, he must attempt to control everything in his life, leaving nothing to chance. Such an individual is very responsible and deathly afraid of the unknown. He fears making the wrong choice and losing the little control he has, so he over-plans. He gives everything a specific spot that can't be moved. He tries to live his life as perfectly as possible, based on what he sees others doing because that is all he knows. This kind of victim is also lost in the dark, but he follows the flashlights of others to try and find an exit. Rather than alcohol, he shields himself with attempts to be intellectual and always in control of the situation.

My personality steered me towards the latter.

Knowing this made me question if any of my choices where my own. It made me wonder if the life I chose was really in my control. Do I really love to read, or is that just an auto-defense mechanism to try and have some control over my life when control was taken away from me? Am I really responsible with money, or am I just afraid of making wrong decisions with my money? Am I supposed to be a teacher, or am I meant to be in LA or New York making it as a professional actor? All of these questions have gone through my head. I even question whether or not I was supposed to be married to Sarah or whether it was my mind choosing to date white women all these years because it was a black girl that raped me. What was the truth?

There is one thing I do know after dwelling and meditating on the issue: this is the life I've chosen. The friends I have, the family I have created, and the life I've built was done by me. And it's because of this life that I have changed and helped the lives of many young people I have taught, coached, and come in contact with. It's because of this life that I have a lovely daughter that makes me smile and brings peace to the people she meets. In the beginning, I may not have had a choice over my life. Something may have been taken away that altered the way I saw the world, but I could have chosen to drown my problems in cigarettes and alcohol rather than a long run and self-reflection. There was another option, and I chose the more responsible one. That means something. So, whether I act too white, or if I'm not black enough, means nothing when compared to the fact that I'm me, and that's all that truly matters— at least that's all that matters to me now. Before, being black meant something much, much, *much* different.

Gay or Marry a White Woman

It all began in the nineties.

It was the R&B golden age of silk shirts, Captain Planet, and TGIF. They were ten years of adolescence spent walking the halls of

Woodrow Wilson Elementary and Sterling Middle in Peoria, Illinois, in which I questioned (and hated) each and every thing about each and every thing, like every other preteen that came before and will come after.

No matter your age, gender, ethnicity, blood type, or sperm count, you know it's true. From age seven to whenever we decide the world isn't out to get us, we hate ourselves, our parents, teachers, school, school mascot, world, town, city, color of the sky, taste of pears, air we breathe, and everything else we can and can't see. For ten (or fifty) years, we figure out what makes us tick—our likes, tolerances, and dislikes. We make friends, create enemies, remember nothing learned in the classroom, but feel every misplaced word pointed in our direction as a crime against humanity. During these years, our bodies change. Boys search desperately for facial (and pubic) hair, girls search for bumps to become boobs, and all that matters is where the next pimple will make its next surprise appearance.

It seems impossible at the time, but most of us get through it with only minimal mental scars and vivid memories of a girl's bra strap showing through her T-shirt two seats ahead and thinking, *There are boobs in there.* (I know I wasn't the only one.) What do you expect? For ten years, we're brain dead. We're walking zombies governed by hormones, gently moaning, "That's not fair. That's not fair," while sucking our teeth in disgust. The Fred Savage years are the worst years of our life, no exception. But for me, they meant finding out what it meant to be black.

I don't mean black like "Is she dark-skinned like Rudy on *The Cosby Show*, or light-skinned like Whitley on *A Different World*," but like "You're black, so you can dunk, right?" Black meant how cool you were, and if you were a nerd, it was a question that came up every 2.3 seconds (like the bra strap). Although the question came and went over the years, there were two small but impressionable events that made me question my blackness above all the other name calling and tears that surfaced throughout the years.

The first was at my grandmother's house in York, Alabama.

Before I continue, I would like to paint a picture of this small Alabama town. Then, the town was Mayberry, if Mayberry had black people. It consisted of two gas stations (one right across from the other), a convenience store called The Log Cabin that sold the best Bomb Pops (aka red-white-and blue popsicles), and a Church's Fried Chicken. It was the kind of place where everyone waved when they saw you drive down the street, because they figured if you were there, they must know you or be related to you. People left their houses and cars unlocked and had no fear that, when they returned, everything would be in its place. It was a nice town, but boring beyond belief. Watching the grass grow was an *actual* pastime, along with watching the paint dry, kicking the can, and any other old-school southern clichés you can think of. I can only assume that it's because of the boredom that my grandparents ended up having twelve children. You have to do something to pass the time.

The year was 1995. I was ten and at my grandparent's house known simply by everyone as "The Hill." Everyone called it The Hill because the one-room shack my grandfather had built and pieced together into a fourteen-room house sat on top of a huge hill surrounded by about ten acres of farmland, pigs, forest, and a partial junkyard. It's where my grandmother farmed, my grandfather raised and slaughtered pigs, and my uncles and aunts worked on cars in their heyday. A few of them still sat in the yard and around the house collecting weeds, rust, dirt, and grass (the cars, not my aunts and uncles).

It was August, and after a twelve-hour drive, we were back for our annual weeklong supposed vacation/boring family visit.

It was morning and all my uncles and aunts had come to The Hill for breakfast. They sat at the kitchen table talking, laughing, and making fun of each other like they always did when they all came together. I was just waking up and moving from the back bedroom of the house, to the kitchen, when I heard one of my uncles say through the cracks of the door separating the kitchen from the back rooms of the house, "Either Kenny's going to be gay when he grows up or marry a white woman." Everyone laughed, clapped, and slapped their knee at its hilarity and how it wasn't, but was, but wasn't (but really was) true.

I don't remember if my mom or Aunt Jackie stuck up for me, but I do remember feeling pretty crappy, wondering why I wasn't black as I made my way to the bathroom rather than the kitchen. I didn't ask why they didn't *see* me as being black, or why I didn't *feel* or *act* black, but why I *wasn't* black. The thought and feeling has yet to fully vanish. It's a thought that often comes when I'm around family. Hell, the first and only real words I remember my grandfather saying to or about me was, "If Kenny ever went and talked to a girl, he would say, 'Hi,'" he pretended to take two puffs of an imaginary inhaler, "'you wanna go out?'" Everyone always laughs and calls these jokes, but they are really a reflection of their version of the truth.

The second incident happened three years later. I was in eighth grade and loved to run but was cursed with asthma (as my grandfather knew as well) any time I ran more than a block. I've had asthma all my life, but that was the first time I was able to get medication to treat my symptoms when they popped up. I had just come back from my first doctor's appointment and was very excited, giddy to say the least, with the new medication I had been given (Advair, Diskus, and Singulair). I had gone to the bathroom skipping and singing "A Whole New World" in preparation for the upcoming Children's Community Theatre audition (no joke), to read the directions and take my first dose of sweet savior, when I heard my sister say to Mom, "I've never seen someone so excited to take medication before." I cried, my sister apologized, and everyone moved on, except me.

It didn't have quite the impact as my uncle implying that I wasn't black, but it hurt more because it came from someone immediate. It implied I was different from other people like me and that I needed to behave "normally" in order to be socially accepted.

Both incidents made me not only wonder who I was (as the wonder years are supposed to do), but why I wasn't black, normal, and able to fit in.

In the nineties, and in many ways now, *black* was not a color; it was a way of being and behaving. In the mind of an adolescent black boy who always felt like an outsider, looking over the rim of his glasses toward the socialites, being black meant you had to prove your "blackness." This meant acting and looking *black*. So, in order to figure out how to fit in and be more black, I created a mental checklist I needed to complete sometime before the end of my life in order to become as black as (if not blacker than) Shaft. I created this list after studying my brother (who I thought was the coolest person alive), TV shows, music videos, movies, friends, relatives, enemies that always seemed to take the girl I liked (I still hate you, SJ), and what fragments of information I could get from the science fiction and fantasy books that occupied most of my time. The checklist went as follows:

Step 1: Basketball is key! Every socially accepted black boy I had ever met knew how to play basketball. They played for a team, could shoot three-pointers, make layups, watched it on TV, but more importantly, could dribble the ball between their legs. In my mind, this was the coolest thing in the world. It was modern magic to be able to move from bouncing a ball with one hand to bouncing it with the other through outstretched legs without it hitting you in the balls (as it always did with me). In my head, if I was going to be black, I had to play basketball. You didn't have to play football, but you had to know the rules, which I knew nothing about. I still don't.

Step 2: Look good, no matter what. Being black meant looking good all the time. Your hair was always cut and faded, and the clothes you bought were always new and brand name (Nike, Jordan, K-Swiss, Nautica, Tommy Hilfiger, Polo). This also meant you always looked cool. Whether it was sipping a can of soda or walking down the driveway, you always looked cool. Words came out as smooth as the silk shirts I begged my mother to buy for me.

Step 3: Black girlfriend! This was the most difficult and most important. Achieving step three would mean I had made it. I had to somehow, against all odds, be transformed from Steve Urkel into Stephon Arkel. Somehow, I had to be dowsed in a poorly-labeled container of toxic waste and emerge transformed into the new-and-improved, more-powerful, more-cool, more-black, Super Kenny, blacker, stronger, and more attractive than any adaptation of Shaft (Samuel L. Jackson, Michael Cira, or any other).

It was only a dream, because I had a weakness like supercharged kryptonite constantly working against me—the nerd checklist:

Step 1: Reading books is awesome! I loved books! I still love books, especially science fiction and fantasy. Reading a book a day in middle school for the Accelerated Reader Program was not cool. Writing short stories for the young author submission was not cool. I couldn't put the books away. As Pookie said in the movie *New Jack City*, "They just keep callin' me, man. They just keep callin' me." No matter how hard I tried and how many new clothes I bought, I couldn't make reading a book look cool.

Step 2: Oops! If you've ever seen *The Goonies*, you know Chunk. There's a scene in the movie in which all the kids are in the basement hiding from the Fratellis and looking for the secret entrance to One-Eyed Willie's treasure, when Chunk starts yelling that they all need to leave. In the middle of his rant, he runs into a watercooler, grabs the base, and tries to keep it from falling to the ground, but it's too late. It hits the floor, shatters into a million pieces, and in unison everyone says, "You klutz!" That, ladies and gentlemen, was me trying to dribble a basketball down an empty court, let alone between my legs. It was impossible.

Step 3: I was ugly! On top of everything else, I was ugly. What I didn't know was that every middle school student is ugly. It's true, there are some gods and goddesses of middle school who are gorgeous, but they are few and far between. Everyone else looks up at Mount Olympus from far below and wonders what ambrosia tastes like. All normal middle schoolers have limbs out of proportion, zits that appear overnight, and smells wafting from orifices that secrete juices that you thought only appeared in D-rated horror movies. It can't be helped. All anyone can do is keep breathing until high school, when you can get muscles and grow into your body. Until then, you're at the mercy of the preteen gods.

This was me. I was/am a nerd. There is nothing I could do to make myself more black, so I gave in. I embraced it. I did what I liked rather than what was expected. I ran cross country, became a drama geek, read books that weren't assigned, did speech and debate, and listened to Jason Mraz and John Mayer. I knew I wasn't behaving very *black*, but I was happy. Eventually, I stopped noticing the stares and the comments, because they went away, or they didn't matter anymore. High school and college came and went, and eventually, over time, I became me.

However, this idea of being black stays with me nevertheless and still leaves me questioning, *Am I black enough?* And the answer is no, I'm not, because being black doesn't matter when it compares to being a good husband and a good father.

My uncle was right, sort of. In his eyes, I did marry a white woman rather than a beautiful dark-skinned African queen, as they would say. However, in my eyes, I married my best friend, the college roommate with whom I shared an apartment while she was engaged to another man (that's an entirely different story for another time). I married the person with whom I knew I could spend the rest of my life and raise a family. I could be happy to laugh, cry, read, watch bad movies, and just sit around and do nothing with her until I die. I love my wife and the life we have built together. I love my children more than I could ever myself. Everything I do and decide is for them. These things don't make me black, but they make me a good man, and that's something of which I am far prouder. Being black never meant loving Sarah any less or dampening the pain of miscarrying our first child, even if I can't dribble a basketball between my legs. And if there's one thing I've learned from being in an interracial relationship, it's that, no matter the skin color, love is colorless, and the woman is always right.

Part Three
Becoming the Villain:
Consequences of Neglecting
Trauma Stewardship

"Everyone resents someone. An adversary. A colleague. Even a friend. But to harbor such resentment and bury it deep makes it dangerous. Under the wrong circumstances what might have been dealt with as a ripple builds to a tidal wave. Left in its wake is only devastation."

—**The Spectre**, *Justice League #44*, "Cold War Part One: Monster Within" (2020)

The journey of a hero is very similar to a caregiver's journey of healing. Similar to Joseph Campbell's description of a fictional character's path of leaving their place of birth in hopes of becoming a hero in his book *Hero of a Thousand Faces*, caregivers begin their Call to Adventure by leaving the safety of their Paradise Island and venturing down the path of learning to help survivors of sexual abuse heal from their childhood trauma. Unfortunately, while helping survivors, some caregivers lose a sense of who they are as individuals due to the impact of listening to the trauma of others. The scales of work and life tip disproportionately out of balance, causing caregivers to begin experiencing valleys of sadness and confusion while struggling to acquire the skills needed to understand the trauma of those who have been victimized. These periods are dark and seem to last an eternity as caregivers wait for a survivor to reach a breakthrough in understanding the impact their childhood sexual assault has had on their life in the past and in the present. This period of time is categorized as the **Abyss**.

Following these dark moments of feeling lost and unsure of their actions as a caregiver, there are peaks of joy and bliss when the pieces of the puzzle begin to fit together for survivors and the scale of work, life, and happiness suddenly tip in the other direction. Unlike the seeming longevity of the Abyss, these periods of happiness are brief and known as the **Apotheosis**.

Knowing what it means to experience these highs and lows on your journey of healing as a professional caregiver or loved one of a survivor can be difficult to understand. However, Wonder Woman's journey as a hero in the first twenty-five issues of DC comic's *Wonder Woman: Rebirth* can offer a sense of guidance.

Diana first demonstrates what it means to experience the longevity of sadness caused by the Abyss, illustrating what it may mean for caregivers, in *Wonder Woman #1*. In this comic, she realizes she has been denied from returning to the place of her birth, Themyscira. The knowledge of losing connection to her home places Diana into a state of depression, causing her to experience a mental breakdown, sinking further into the Abyss. While attempting to recover from a sense of sadness in a mental health facility, Diana loses her good friend, Dr. Barbara Ann Minerva, to the villain Cheetah for the second time on her journey as a hero.

Finally, in 2017's *Wonder Woman #24* "Godwatch: Epilogue," Diana loses the Golden Perfect after realizing her way home has forever denied her access, forcing her to sink to the depths of despair, believing escape from this feeling an impossibility. The impact of the truth about her past and the loss of her home, her friend, and the Golden Perfect all cause Diana to lose sight of who she is as an individual and what she represents as Wonder Woman, in the same way caregivers can lose sight of who they are as individuals when helping survivors battle their traumatic past.

Filled with anger and resentment, Diana confronts the ancient Greek gods who gave her the golden truth lasso, the Perfect, and blessed her with the superhuman abilities of Wonder Woman. Diana tells Athena that she has been wronged and deserves better treatment from the patrons she once trusted. In response, Athena does not grow angry. Instead, she asks the heroine:

> *Do you think? But you have everything you ever dreamed of! The girl who wondered has seen wonders has become a woman who has traveled the world, who has traveled worlds! A woman who has touched countless lives, has made them better in ways beyond measure. A woman who has brought hope, and joy, and love. A woman who is the hero of love. A woman who is the hero of so many. The truth of you has never changed, Diana. Even the gods themselves could not take that from you.*

Afterward, Diana looks into her reflection, and the Golden Perfect reappears at her side. From that moment on, the shroud of anger and resentment lifts, and Wonder Woman enters the Apotheosis.

Although the comic ends on a pleasant note with Steve Trevor and Diana asleep in each other's arms, in reality a balanced life cannot be achieved by experiencing the ebbs and flows of emotion caused by the Abyss and the Apotheosis. Without practicing trauma stewardship, the daily trials of a caregiver can lead to long valleys of anger as a result of the Abyss followed by short peaks of joy caused by the Apotheosis. Without maintaining a sense of *who* you are, rather than *what* you do, the impact of harboring the trauma of survivors will affect the relationships you build with others in the same way the grandiosity Diana attaches to being Wonder Woman eventually affects her relationship with Steve Trevor.

This part of the book explores the impact of trauma exposure and the negative response to its effects that can occur over time by caregivers who do not practice trauma stewardship. Laura van Dernoot Lipsky defines **trauma exposure response** in her book *Trauma Stewardship* as the transformation that takes place within a caregiver as a result of exposure to the suffering of other living beings or the planet. The development of a trauma exposure response as a caregiver is a result of compounding psychological, physical, and behavioral stress at work and sometimes at home. According to Martha Teater and John Ludgate in their workbook *Overcoming Compassion Fatigue,* some common symptoms of caregiver stress and burnout are:

Psychological

- Being easily frustrated
- Irritability
- Annoyance
- Isolation
- Sadness
- Feeling inadequate or ineffective
- Negativity
- Intrusive thoughts or images related to someone's suffering

- Preoccupation
- Difficulty feeling tender, warm, experiencing intimate emotions
- Detachment
- Anger at perpetrator or causal event
- Guilt
- Loss of a sense of personal safety and control
- Feeling more vulnerable to danger
- Depersonalizing others
- Sense of humor becomes darker, more cynical, or sarcastic
- Negative self-image
- Depressive symptoms
- Reduced empathy
- Resentment
- Less pleasure in work

Physical
- Headaches
- Stomach complaints
- Muscle tension
- Increased blood pressure
- Elevated blood sugar
- Fatigue and exhaustion
- Sleep problems
- Increased susceptibility to illness

Behavioral
- Hyper-alertness
- Restless

- Jumpy
- Nervous
- Easily startled
- Hyper-vigilance
- Change in response to violence: numbed or increased sensitivity
- Difficulty thinking clearly
- Trouble making decisions
- Greater use of alcohol or other drugs
- Reduced sex drive
- Anger
- Exaggerated sense of responsibility
- Forgetfulness
- Difficulty with personal relationships

At Work

- Feeling overwhelmed by client needs
- Decreased commitment to work
- Resentment toward employer
- Increased tardiness or absences
- Poor boundaries
- Work life and personal life bleed into each other
- Less compassion toward those you serve
- Over-functioning
- See yourself as being indispensable

Recognizing your trauma exposure response and its effect on your feelings, thoughts, and behaviors as a caregiver is one of the first steps toward balancing the scales of life, work, and stable mental health in the form of practicing effective trauma stewardship.

Chapter Eight
Grandiosity of Wonder Woman
and the Loss of Diana

"The purpose of war is to end conflict."

—**Ares**, *Wonder Woman # 195*, "The Mission" (2003)

Themyscira is located on Paradise Island, an island of harmony and perfection where, on its surface, its Amazonian inhabitants work and live in peace with one another and nature. However, beneath its surface, in the deep, dark depths of the island, the perfection and beauty of Themyscira fades. Locked away in its caverns lay unspeakable evils, and the Amazons are its jailers. To understand why Wonder Woman's home is a place of both beauty and danger requires an understanding of the responsibility placed on the shoulders of each Amazon warrior by the Greek gods after turning away from the role as ambassadors of peace and creating a grandiose view of themselves and their way of life as warriors of Paradise Island.

Amazon warriors did not originate on Themyscira. In fact, they were not born warriors at all. They were born as women whose lives were cut short due to the fear-filled and hateful actions of men throughout time. Before passing into the afterlife, each soul was saved and protected in the Cavern of Souls by the titan, Gaea, to eventually be reborn as Amazons by the Greek goddesses Athena, Artemis, Hestia, Demeter, and Aphrodite.

Once resurrected, these women did not live on an island veiled and separated from the world of men. Instead, they governed a city-state, where they attempted to show the world how to lead with compassion, love, and justice, as directed to do so by their Greek goddess patrons. In "The Princess and the Power" (1987), when the five goddesses look down on the women from the clouds above, they say:

> *You are a chosen race, born to lead humanity in the ways of virtue, the way of Gaea! Through you, all men shall know us better. And worship us always! Therefore does Athena grant you wisdom, that you may be guided by the light of truth and justice! I, Artemis, grant you skill in the hunt! Hestia shall build you a city and warm your hearths, and it is fair Aphrodite who grants you the great gift of love! Forevermore, you shall find strength in these gifts. They are your most sacred birthright—they are your power! You, Hippolyte, shall be queen over all my daughters! Antiope, you shall rule by your sister's side! See to it that these gifts we give are never abused! And wear you both these symbols of our trust— Gaea's Girdle! Never let it be removed! Now go, daughters! Henceforth, you shall form a sacred sisterhood! Henceforth, you shall be Amazons! And none may resist your power!*

Unfortunately, rather than acceptance and understanding by the established patriarch of Greece, the Amazons are treated as outcasts and feared by their male counterparts. Fueled by the rage of Ares, the Amazon city-state is attacked by the demigod Herakles and his men. Following his defeat in battle with Queen Hippolyta, Herakles yields, feigns peace, poisons the queen, removes Gaea's Girdle, and enslaves the Amazon warriors.

Beaten but not broken, Queen Hippolyta seeks rescue from her captors, praying to Athena for salvation and forgiveness. Instead, the Greek goddesses grant Hippolyta the strength to free herself from captivity, but only after warning the Amazonian queen that "Bloody vengeance is not the answer, daughter! It is time for you to cleanse your soul, time to rededicate yourself to that which Gaea gave you! Only then shall you be free!"

Although Hippolyta heeds Athena's words, freeing herself without the use of bloodshed, her Amazonian sisters do not. Rather than take their male captors prisoner, they kill them, disobeying the words of warning by Athena. To pay penance for losing their way as leaders of wisdom and compassion in a world of men, the Amazons are forced onto Paradise Island as eternal jailers of an unspeakable evil locked away beneath its surface. To remind them of their past and ensure history does not repeat itself, they wear their bracelets of bondage. It is on Paradise Island that the Amazons build a new Themyscira, perfect but always housing unspeakable horrors below its surface.

Later, when a portion of this evil is released following the death of Ares, Paradise Island is rocked to its core, destroying Mount Olympus and bringing ancient mythical creatures to Earth. When this occurs, Diana believes it is her responsibility alone as Wonder Woman to restore order to Themyscira and Mount Olympus and find a way to contain the released titans. Unfortunately, Diana's grandiose view of her need to set things right as Wonder Woman without the help of others eventually leads to the destruction of her relationship with Steve Trevor, the loss of her powers, and a lack of understanding of herself as an Amazon.

This chapter explores how sometimes you as a caregiver behave in the same manner as Diana. The grandiose view of your profession as a guide who helps survivors of childhood sexual abuse heal from their trauma may lead you toward becoming unable to maintain your trauma stewardship in a balanced way that encourages establishing healthy boundaries that separate work and personal relationships. Diana's loss of her love, friends, and super abilities will help provide context in understanding how a grandiose view of never being, or doing, enough as a caregiver can lead to burnout, compassion fatigue, and secondary traumatic stress.

Grandiosity

For caregivers of survivors of childhood sexual abuse, there is always something more that needs to be done in an attempt to help trauma survivors move along their journey of healing. They know the impact of their job as a caregiver can sometimes have life-or-death consequences, and it is for this reason many believe that what they do in their job is never enough. They push themselves to the brink while simultaneously pushing those they care for, and who care for them, away in the process, believing their needs and wants can wait until a more convenient time. These caregivers view their profession as **grandiose,** an inflated sense of importance that they are the only ones capable of solving complex problems involving the lives of others they seek to help.

One problem with grandiose views as a caregiver is that it is a trauma exposure response that is a result of behaving and interacting with others under the belief that there will always be time available to accomplish tasks not directly related to helping trauma survivors heal. Unfortunately, this view as a caregiver means emergencies will always arise in need of being attended. Laura van Dernoot Lipsky explains in *Trauma Stewardship* how some caregivers who view their profession as grandiose sometimes become hooked on involvement in the lives of survivors, solving their problems, and becoming increasingly attached to feelings of being needed and useful as a savior rather than a guide.

Another problem with grandiosity is that, as a society, we believe that remaining still equates to being lazy. We believe we must always be moving, working, or doing something that proves our worth in comparison to the accomplishments and possessions of others. It is for this reason you may never feel as though you are worthy of holding a position as a caregiver. You may believe you are living the life of an imposter rather than a balanced existence where you live in the moment. Until caregivers make the decision to practice trauma stewardship, the impact of helping other trauma survivors without taking time for themselves can lead to detrimental consequences.

Grandiosity becomes a problem in the healing journey of a caregiver when the caregiver is not firmly grounded in a larger reality of building healthy relationships, habits, and balance outside their role of helping trauma survivors heal. Viewing your actions as a caregiver as never being enough, the profession as grandiose, and yourself consistently underqualified means viewing your ability to help survivors of trauma as an obligation rather than a fulfilling profession you feel qualified to hold. Focusing on one part of life, such as being an advocate and support system for survivors, compromises other portions of life that become underdeveloped from neglect in the same way Diana compromises her relationship with Steve Trevor. Diana's restricted view of herself and her actions through the lens of Wonder Woman, rather than as an ambassador, friend, lover, and individual with her own needs and wants, causes her to lose her connection to the love and compassion needed to help herself and others.

Grandiosity Leads to the Loss of Love

In *Wonder Woman #76,* "Mothers and Children" (2019), Diana successfully escapes the Abyss of sadness and despair created when Ares, the god of war, is killed, disconnecting Themyscira and Mount Olympus from their realms, and sending mythical beasts to Earth in *Wonder Woman #58,* "The Just War: Part 1" (2018). She successfully reaches an Apotheosis of relief after rediscovering a connection to Themyscira and restoring balance to Mount Olympus. Unfortunately, the joy does not last. In a single day, Diana plunges back into the depths of despair after discovering her former friend, Dr. Barbara Ann Minerva, and current villain, Cheetah, has killed Aphrodite using a sword known as God Killer.

Following the death of love, Diana experiences the shattering of her relationship with Steve Trevor, a disconnect from her abilities as Wonder Woman, and the loss of her weapons. In the same way the death of Aphrodite and the loss of love throughout the world brought Diana to her knees, grandiosity causes caregivers to lose the love of their profession, resulting in the shattering of their relationships and loss of self as a caregiver.

Loss of Love Leads to a Deterioration of Healthy Relationships

The impact of grandiosity resulting in the loss of love can first be seen in the deterioration of the romantic relationship between Diana and Steve. It is common knowledge that the relationship between Diana Prince and Steve Trevor is complicated. Diana loves Steve, but she places her duties as Wonder Woman above her relationship. Although she is consistently flying away to save the day and protect those unable to protect themselves, Steve remains patient and understanding. He knows the importance of Diana's job as Wonder Woman, just as she knows the importance of his job as soldier in the United States military to combat crime and evil at home and abroad. However, although Steve is understanding of Diana's continued absence as she works tirelessly to restore Themyscira and Mount Olympus, eventually he decides there is only so long he can wait for his angel to grace him with her presence.

When beginning to restore order to Mount Olympus and discover what has happened to Themyscira following the paradox caused by the death of Ares, Steve is encouraging and understanding of Diana's need to discover the truth about what has happened to her home. In *Wonder Woman #64*, "The Grudge" (2019), as Diana races to retrieve her weapons for battle, Steve waits at the door, places them in her hands, and with a smile and kiss on the head tells her, "Go. Save the world. I love you."

Later, Steve's patience and understanding begins to wane as he waits and worries for Diana to return. Standing on the deck of their home, Aphrodite asks Steve if he ever tires of waiting for Diana to make time for him in her life. He responds, "I mean, yeah, I get tired of it. The waiting around. But I never get tired of her. And she needs me—she needs somebody to wait here on this balcony for her to come home. Sometimes, I think she might forget this is home, otherwise."

Steve's words are not only true for the relationship between Diana and himself, but the relationship between many caregivers who view themselves and their actions as those of a savior rather than a guide for survivors. The lovers and partners of caregivers sometimes view their need to stay and wait as an obligation to the person they love, rather than a choice. Similar to the way Steve knows Wonder Woman's job is crucial in the fight against evil, loved ones know the work of their caregiver is important when helping others heal from past trauma. Understanding creates less of a problem when not being placed first in their caregiver's life.

These loved ones know first-hand how thoughts of grandiosity and feelings they can never be enough continuously race through their minds as a caregiver in the same way Wonder Woman's thoughts race to discover what has happened to her home and whether or not she is capable of rising to the challenge. She thinks to herself:

> I try not to spend too much time alone in my own mind. This is how the doubt gets. Yet between the Earth and the sky, where there is only silence, I must live with my thoughts. And I wonder.. . do I have the strength of which Aphrodite seemed so certain? Or am I destined to fail? And when it matters most, will I be able to tell the difference?

Loved ones of caregivers know these thoughts are difficult to manage, but they also wish they were as important as the trauma survivors being helped. If you as a caregiver continue to hold the grandiose views of your job and that what you do is never enough, it can lead to a splitting of relationships until they eventually shatter from the accumulated trauma absorbed from attempting to be a savior to others. Balance can no longer be maintained, and those you care for no longer feel as though they are no longer important in your life as they begin questioning why they wait for someone who never seems to make the time for them, in the same manner Steve Trevor begins to question why he waits for Diana to make time for him.

Later, in *Wonder Woman #77*, as Diana races off to battle, Steve no longer presents the warrior with her weapons and a kiss to the forehead. Instead, he stands in the doorway and sternly asks, "Will there ever a point when I come first? When we come first?" Rather than provide a straightforward answer, she flies away. When Diana does eventually arrive home, weakened, without her Bracelets of Submission and Golden Perfect, Steve tells her,

> *Diana, what we have together is a lot more than love. It's history, it's friendship, it's duty . . . and in a different relationship that might be enough. Heck, plenty of marriages are built on less. But now, if you were around more, you'd have noticed that things have been rocky between us for a while. But now it seems like the reason to stay is gone. Goodbye, Diana. I'll always care about you. But I can't keep putting so much of myself into this and getting so little back.*

Diana is left sitting alone on her bed in bandages and tears. Steve's decision to leave took months of absence by Diana, the destruction of her Bracelets of Submission, and the death of love. Although all of these did occur, it was Diana's belief of the grandiosity of her role as Wonder Woman, and always needing to do more in order to help others that began her journey from Apotheosis into the Abyss. Understanding the consequences of Diana's journey explains how you as a caregiver to survivors of childhood sexual abuse may encounter similar consequences in your relationships.

Loss of Love Leads to a Loss of Self

Grandiosity can lead caregivers down the path of losing the passion for helping survivors of childhood sexual abuse heal in the same manner Diana lost her passion as Wonder Woman. When Cheetah kills Greek goddess Aphrodite in *Wonder Woman #78,* "Loveless: Part 2" (2019), she strips Wonder Woman of the greatest power she did not know she possessed: love. Diana realizes the loss of this crucial asset while battling Cheetah and avenging the murder of Aphrodite. The heroine hesitates to attack the villain, losing the drive to fight and no longer seeing the point in avenging the death of her patron and friend. The loss of love causes Diana's sword to split in two, shield to break, Golden Perfect to be stolen, and Bracelets of Submission to shatter, leaving Diana struggling to stay afloat while drifting downstream bruised and beaten.

Diana describes the impact of love and its loss when she says:

> *Love is dangerous. Love is a wild thing that fights even when death is certain. Love is hope in the face of defeat. And without it . . . without it we are each alone in the universe. Moving past our fellow travelers like ghosts. Love is the last fragment of the will. The one that persists after all other resources are gone.*

The persistence of grandiosity as a caregiver strips the love and passion you may have for helping trauma survivors. Instead of possessing the compassion needed to help survivors of trauma heal, you become filled with resentment, anger, fear, and hatred that begins to fester until love is no longer present, and in its place is burnout, compassion fatigue, and secondary traumatic stress. Diana describes these feelings of hopelessness and loss of love in *Wonder Woman #79,* "Loveless: Part 3" (2019), as strangers rob and attack one another while she sits in the center of the street, thinking:

> *My limbs have turned to sand. They are heavy with the weight of failure. And something else, something I have never felt before . . . perhaps it is shame. I have lost my weapons. I have lost my will . . . and worst of all . . . I have lost the people I came here*

to serve. And yet, somehow, there is still light. Are the gods speaking, giving some hint of what is still to come? No, the gods are dead or have fled their posts. Nothing now stands between us and our worst instincts. And we are all wanderers in our own lands.

Diana is a fictional character in a universe of superheroes and villains that does not exist. However, as a caregiver who consistently views themselves and their actions as never enough in a profession believed to be grandiose in nature, her words may ring true. When drained and unable to perpetuate the false beliefs of caregivers as being selfless heroes who always place the needs of others before themselves, you become filled with shame. You believe hope is lost as you sit on the floor attempting to collect the weapons to combat feelings of sadness.

Rather than make the decision to practice trauma stewardship and recalibrate the need for balance in your life, you attempt to rise and fight the persistent negative feelings of not being enough as a caregiver, in the same manner as Diana in *Wonder Woman #80*, "Loveless: Part 4" (2019). You say to yourself, in the same manner as Wonder Woman:

Love comes and goes. Allies come and go. The work continues. Yet I cannot shake the feeling that I have failed. I forgot what was most important and now it is lost. Yet I cannot linger here on this grief. I get up because I must. Despair is not permitted to me. Love is dead, but the memory of love remains. And it must suffice. For failure is too terrible to contemplate.

Thinking these thoughts only leads to self-destructive tendencies. It is for this reason it is important to remember that you are not Wonder Woman. You are also not a fictional comic book character in a universe of clear-cut, black-and-white rules of good and evil. You are more than a savior for trauma survivors who have suffered childhood sexual abuse. You are a human being with needs, wants, desires, and a life of your own who is allowed to feel a full range of emotions, including sadness. There is only so long we can force ourselves to rise and neglect our feelings in the same manner as Diana before burnout sets in. The impact of continuously being exposed to the trauma of others can lead to despair and the need to lean on others, which is okay. It is okay to need time to heal and regain balance. If you do not allow yourself this time to stop, rest, and reflect, the consequences may lead to the loss of love entirely.

Chapter Nine
Understanding Burnout,
Compassion Fatigue, and
Secondary Traumatic Stress

"How many times, Diana? How many times have you set aside your heart for duty?"

—**Princess Maxima**, *Wonder Woman #754*, "The Truth Usurps" (2020)

In *Sensation Comics Featuring Wonder Woman #1*, "Gothamazon" (2014), Batman is out of commission for a single night. This leaves the streets of Gotham City vulnerable to attack and in need of protection. Rather than call on Superman, Green Lantern, or Flash for assistance, Barbara Gordon calls on Wonder Woman to prevent the Joker, Two Face, Poison Ivy, Mr. Freeze, Penguin and Man Bat from wreaking havoc throughout the streets of Gotham City.

Although these are some the most heinous villains in Batman's Rogues Gallery, the heroine believes her job as Gotham's protector for the night will be simple and the villains will be defeated easily. She believes this because, although Batman is one of the most powerful superheroes in the DC universe, he is still only human, and because she is a superhero with powers similar to those of a god, she believes she will make fast work of the villains. Unfortunately, she is mistaken.

While it is true Wonder Woman has the strength of Superman combined with the tactical training of an Amazon warrior, she must show restraint when using her abilities to ensure she does not harm those she is trying to protect. As a hero who embodies truth, compassion, and honesty, the villains realize they can exploit these strengths as a weakness by being willing to have no regard for human life as they commit crimes. While saving innocent women and children from burning buildings, Diana begins to wonder how Batman battles this level of evil each night while retaining his humanity. She even contemplates dark thoughts of strangling, cutting, and breaking the necks of each villain, realizing how easy it would be to bring the rogues to their knees through the might of her fist rather than the truth of her words.

Wonder Woman knows the villains do not fear her in the same way they fear Batman, but she believes she can make them fear her if she kills them. She narrates to herself, "They fear the man in black. But they don't know the monsters and gods I've put to eternal rest. If I chose monsters, the Bat would seem a blessed reprieve. And before they expired? I would fill them with wonder."

She allows herself only a moment to contemplate murder before remembering her namesake as Truth Queen. Rather than kill her enemies, Diana remains true to herself and her code as an Amazon. She does not use brute force to stop the villains. Instead, she uses the Golden Perfect to allow each villain the opportunity to face the truth of the deepest fears that drive them to hurt others.

By the end of the comic, Wonder Woman captures each villain and Barbara Gordon narrates from her Watchtower as Oracle:

> And I admit it. I was a skeptic. But she really did change Gotham in her image. For a while. Some of the villains she touched went to rehab, and a couple even went straight entirely. Who'da thunk? Even Batman, when he came back, seemed impressed. A little. I wouldn't have thought it likely, but Gotham will miss her. She was strong, but kind and compassionate. Human. And brave.

"Gothamazon" is unique because it shows the dark thoughts of Wonder Woman and the acts of horror she could be capable of if she allowed herself to venture down the rabbit hole of seeking revenge rather than justice. It also helps demonstrate how listening to the traumatic experiences of others can sometimes have a negative effect on caregivers. The act of helping trauma survivors heal from their childhood abuse through the simple act of engaging with the recovery process has the ability to cause the mind to believe it is experiencing trauma firsthand rather than simply listening to someone else's trauma. In the same way Wonder Woman's interaction with Batman's Rogues Gallery transforms her thoughts from those of truth to possibilities of revenge, a caregiver's thoughts and feelings can become hijacked by the experiences of the survivors they help. This is does not mean the thoughts and experiences of a survivor are similar to those of a villain. It only means that harboring the traumatic abuse of a survivor rather than practicing trauma stewardship can lead to negative thoughts, feelings, and actions.

This chapter explores the possible consequences of **burnout, compassion fatigue,** and **secondary traumatic stress** if a caregiver does not put in the time needed to maintain balance and metabolize the emotions they are feeling rather than reacting to their effects.

The Effects of Burnout

Unlike compassion fatigue and secondary traumatic stress, burnout can happen to anyone in any profession, regardless of whether or not they are a caregiver. The restraints and/or demands of a stress-filled job can cause an individual to lose the passion they once had for a career they loved. Burnout can be caused by the implementation of new policies and procedures, the continuation of toxic or dated policies and procedures, the hiring of new administration, or life changes that require the need for more personal time rather than work qualifications no longer capable of being achieved.

In 2018, the American Psychological Association found that between 21 and 61 percent of mental health practitioners experience burnout and that social workers appear to be potentially more burned out than any other human service workers. Researchers, Michael P. Leiter and Christina Maslach find that burnout consists of three components: emotional exhaustion, depersonalization, and feelings of ineffectiveness. It is for this reason that burnout is more difficult to cure than compassion fatigue and secondary traumatic stress. This is because curing burnout can require major organizational changes in culture, policies, and practices.

To determine if you are suffering from burnout, Maslach and Leiter recommend asking yourself these questions:

- Do I feel I have a sustainable workload, or do I feel overloaded with work?

- Do I have a feeling of choice or control in my work environment?

- Do I have a sense of reward and recognition at work?

- Is there a breakdown in the sense of community or belonging in my work environment?

- Do I experience fairness, justice, and respect at work?

- Do I view my work as meaningful and in line with my values?

- Is there a disconnect between who I am as a person and my job?

They claim that "burnout is not a problem of the people themselves but of the social environment in which the people work." To understand the impact of burnout, there is no better example than the burnout of Wonder Woman and a Russian Superman bent on the spread of communism in the graphic novel *Superman: Red Son.*

Wonder Woman, Burnout, and a Russian Superman

Superman: Red Son (2014) is arguably one of the most unique and (in my opinion) coolest graphic novels ever written. In the setting of this alternate universe, Superman does not fight for truth, justice, and the American way. Instead, he is a Soviet Russian fighting to spread communism. While many of the other DC characters are present, their backstory has also been altered in the same manner as Superman. Batman is a Russian who views Superman as a threat to humanity that must be destroyed; Lex Luthor is the president of the United States; and Lois Lane is Lex Luthor's wife. Wonder Woman's origin remains relatively the same, but instead of falling in love with Steve Trevor, when Diana meets Superman for the first time, she is immediately attracted to the superpowered hero who is so similar to herself in abilities and compassion. In fact, she is so convinced in Superman's belief in the spread of communism throughout the world, she leaves Themyscira to be his international peace ambassador. Unfortunately, Superman does not notice the love Diana has for him. He only sees her shared devotion of communism, which she loses one night in Siberia when she is captured by Batman and bound by her golden lasso of truth.

When Superman arrives to save Diana, he is weakened by red sun lamps installed throughout an abandoned military base by Batman, beaten, and trapped in a cellar. From underground, Superman calls for help from Diana, saying:

> *Diana? Can you hear me? Please listen carefully, because what I'm about to ask you is our only chance against him now. As long as I'm trapped here beneath these red sun rays, I'm powerless. But there must be some kind of generator out there providing the electricity, Diana. I need you to find it for me and destroy it. I know breaking the lasso is going to hurt, but there's really no other way we're going to beat him, Diana. We can't let Batman destroy everything we've ever worked for, and you're the only person now who can get us out of this mess. Please. More*

than anything I've ever asked for before, I need you to help me here, Diana. As your oldest and dearest friend I'm begging you to do whatever it takes here.

With these final words, Wonder Woman breaks free of her lasso, destroys the generator, and Superman flies free, defeating Batman. Afterwards, due to Diana breaking free from the lasso of truth, the heroine ages significantly. With inflamed bracelets, an expression of shock, grey hair, and a withered body, she tells Superman, "I . . . I found the generator. Just like you asked me to. And tossed it into the Norwegian Sea. But I think I might have hurt myself when you made me snap that cord. It was like, I don't know, something just kind of switched off in my head or something."

This scene in the comic literally depicts Diana as being burned out by the demands and selfish views of Superman to shatter truth. Although she was alive and Superman unharmed, from that moment onward, she resented Superman for what he had forced her to do. For weeks she laid in a bed in Moscow as she battled depression and the reality of what it means to be burned out.

The consequences of Diana acting in the better interest of someone other than herself is an excellent example of how burnout occurs due to the constant demand of caregivers being viewed as selfless heroes rather than as individuals with limitations, needs, wants, loves, and dislikes the same as anyone else. In *Red Son*, Superman pushing Diana to do the impossible and commit an act of selflessness that would have severe consequences is the equivalent of a job that continuously does not make the needs and concerns of their employees a priority. When this occurs, caregivers end up sacrificing their health and well-being for the good of the cause or organization.

Burnout can also be a result of policies put into place that make it difficult to help survivors in ways that is more beneficial and time sensitive. While the bureaucracy of the system has its benefits in allowing due process, sometimes this system can stand in the way of providing survivors with the help, support, and safety they need to heal. The frustration of continuously having to navigate through layers of red tape can drive professional caregivers to question whether the love they have for helping others is worth the agony of knowing more could have been done if circumstances were different.

Placing the needs of an organization before your own can eventually lead to resentment in the same way Diana came to resent Superman for pushing her toward idolizing his goals of communism rather than prioritizing her safety and health. Without proper management of trauma stewardship that maintains balancing not only the needs of trauma survivors, but the pressures to push one's self beyond healthy limits to be and do more, generates false grandiosity associated with being a professional caregiver.

Battling an oppressive work environment can lead to symptoms of burnout as a trauma exposure response, such as:

Chronic exhaustion: After breaking her lasso and being unable to leave her bed, speak, or move for a number of weeks, Diana exhibits this trauma exposure response. Similar to Diana, caregivers who exhibit chronic exhaustion feel as though no matter how much sleep they obtain, feeling rested is an impossibility. This could be because of feelings of depression or anxiety constantly being battled internally by the caregiver. Similar to Wonder Woman, caregivers find it difficult to find the motivation, let alone the strength, to accomplish the tasks that used to bring them so much joy.

Anger and Guilt: When experiencing burnout, it is common for caregivers to experience feelings of anger and / or guilt. Diana exhibits these effects when she returns to Themyscira. While speaking with Lois Lane Luthor, she expresses her anger in believing in the false ideals of communism perpetuated by Superman. She tells Lois, with disgust in her face and hatred in her heart:

Superman had a clearness in his eyes which I thought separated him from the rest of his gender. But the truth is that he's just as dangerous and power obsessed as any other male. A fact, I regret, that I learned to my cost some years ago. He's a very charismatic individual, and his apparent sincerity fooled me for a long time. If you've ever met him in the flesh, you'll understand how his skin almost crackles.

Diana's anger even pushes her to lead a battalion of Amazons to kill Superman. Anger as a result of burnout can cause caregivers to become filled with hatred toward the actions of their administrators or the bureaucracy of the system that creates so many obstacles when attempting to help trauma survivors heal. This is the same anger that drives Diana to fight the man she would have died to protect only to realize he would not have done the same for her. Diana also exhibits guilt when she blames herself for not noticing the shortsightedness of Superman before it is too late. Caregivers are similar to Diana when blaming themselves for the cause of a survivor's problems or the issues of the organization they work for.

Cynicism: Although similar to anger, cynicism is a trauma response that intensifies beliefs that everything will turn out for the worse no matter what a caregiver accomplishes. Diana exhibits cynicism when she tells Lois Lane Luthor, "Man's world grows more insane with every passing year, Mrs. Luthor. It's only right that a place exists where women can be safe from their vulgarity and all-consuming lust." This is the same heroine that left Themyscira as a young woman in hopes of helping others live life with the clarity and focus of her Amazonian sisters. Following the incident with her lasso, she believes man's world is irredeemable. Caregivers who suffer burnout sometimes exhibit the same negative beliefs in an attempt to contain the bottled anger they feel. The joy and hope they felt when leaving their own Paradise Island is now replaced with the sophisticated trauma exposure response of cynicism.

If burnout continues over a long enough period of time, it can become worse, transforming into compassion fatigue.

The Effects of Compassion Fatigue

Compassion fatigue is the middle ground between burnout and secondary traumatic stress that shares many common characteristics as burnout. Similar to burnout, the effects of compassion fatigue happen over a period of time rather than all at once. However, unlike burnout, compassion fatigue is a condition specific to caring for others who have experienced trauma or challenging conditions. What makes compassion fatigue so unique and detrimental to professional caregivers and loved ones of survivors of childhood trauma seeking to help them heal is that an individual may suffer from burnout and secondary traumatic stress at the same time.

The best way to describe compassion fatigue is having a reduced amount of compassion and caring for those who have been victimized. Unlike burnout, compassion fatigue has less to do with the culture and work environment of a professional caregiver and more to do with frustration and resentment for survivors and their avoidance toward healing.

Due to the cognitive distortions caused as a result of C-PTSD explained in "Part Two: Becoming A Hero," survivors of childhood sexual abuse may know what needs to be done to heal, but are resistant due to past victimization and negative learned behavior. The behavior of these survivors may include addiction to drugs, alcohol, sex, or self-harm in the form of cutting, thoughts of suicide, and/or possible attempts at suicide. Working with survivors over a long period of time can cause the caregiver to view those they are trying to help as the cause of their misfortunes. Compassion fatigue forces caregivers to lose the love of helping others heal, creating a distorted view in which the caregiver views survivors as villains. Wonder Woman exhibits compassion fatigue when she is viewed as a failure as an ambassador of peace by her Amazonian sister in the graphic novel *Kingdom Come.*

Compassion Fatigue and Kingdom Come

Kingdom Come (1996) by Alex Ross and Mark Waid is a graphic novel that is both beautifully drawn and well written. It also offers an excellent example of compassion fatigue with the development of Wonder Woman's character.

The novel is set in the future where heroes such as Superman, Batman, Green Lantern, Flash, and Aquaman have all grown old. In this reality, Earth has become overridden with metahumans and a less compassionate view for those who have committed crimes has set in throughout humanity. Instead of incarceration and rehabilitation for villains who commit heinous crimes, people now demand the crime fit the punishment. When Superman refuses to alter his dated views of truth and justice for the modern age, he retires as a superhero. However, when millions of people die due to the negligence of its current inexperienced superpowered heroes, the Big Blue Boy Scout comes out of retirement to reestablish the Justice League. All metahumans who refuse to comply with his new rules but still use their powers are placed in a maximum facility prison known as the Gulag.

Similar to *Red Son,* in this alternate future, Diana is Superman's second-in-command. However, unlike *Red Son*, it is Diana who loses her sense of humanity and compassion. As the novel progresses toward its climax and Wonder Woman reveals she is no longer the Amazon ambassador of peace, she tells Superman:

> *For years, I had been the Amazon's ambassador to the outside world. My mission was to spread a message of peace and order. As the world continued to darken, there was some doubt as to how well I had done my job. My Amazon sisters . . . my own mother . . . came to suggest that I had perhaps failed. They actually put me on trial. I pled my case, but in the end they*

decreed that I had indeed not changed man's world. That it had changed me. They stripped me of my royalty and my heritage.

Following this decree from her sisters, Diana becomes sterner rather than compassionate towards those who commit crimes. She uses less love to heal her adversaries and more steel to conquer them into submission as she convinces Superman and the other heroes that metahuman prisoners who revolt while incarcerated may need to be killed rather than peacefully put into submission. Her hostility and anger grows until she pierces the heart of superpowered metahuman Von Bach with her sword, killing him during an uprising in the Gulag. Afterward, she tells Batman, "He left me no choice. They began this. I will finish it. We're here to force peace! We're left with no choice! If you stand in the way, I will remove you!"

Diana's growing lack of compassion for those she views as a threat in the form of compassion fatigue is a result of her unacknowledged burnout as Wonder Woman. Her words and actions are a clear example of reacting with the trauma exposure responses of:

- **Service rationing:** This is when a caregiver limits services and resources for those who they believe are worthy of receiving help. Diana exhibits this with her belief that justice, compassion, and love is not for those who refuse to comply when she tells Superman, "We are at war, Kal . . . They're not our kind. We're protectors of humanity. They are barely human." Rather than see everyone as being capable of achieving greatness, Diana views the new heroes as lesser and not worthy of her guidance. She believes her skills and time are only meant for those she deems worthy.

  Caregivers who begin to suffer compassion fatigue view the trauma survivors who practice avoidance and are resistant toward healing as being incapable of healing. They begin to ration their time and resources only for those who are more compliant, because of the belief that if everyone was helped there would not be enough time and resources to go around. This is a trauma response put into place in an attempt to limit the impact of burnout. Unfortunately, this remedy is only a band-aid, and the caregiver begins to view their profession and the trauma survivors they help through a lens of cynicism.

- **Minimization and Numbing:** When caregivers use minimization as a trauma exposure response, current situations are trivialized and viewed as not as important as others. This is because, in the mind of the caregiver, things are not as bad as they could be, or not as dire as another individual's struggles. Diana exhibits this while sitting in space confiding in Superman how she was stripped of her heritage for showing too much compassion and not enough strength when dealing with her enemies. Superman tells Diana that he always admired her gentility. However, instead of accepting the compliment, Diana minimizes her actions and the people she saved over the course of her years as Wonder Woman when she says, "It didn't get the job done," and asking, "Then why isn't the world better?"

  Suffering compassion fatigue often forces caregivers to view their actions as not being enough in the same manner as Diana. They minimize their actions, believing they are not enough, and nothing they do can change that. In an attempt to cure this trauma exposure response, they may grow sterner, numbing their emotions rather than acknowledging the work they have done as being worthy of praise.

  Without achieving balance as a caregiver, the stress of continuous exposure to trauma can lead to the debilitating effects of secondary traumatic stress, also known as **vicarious trauma.**

Secondary Traumatic Stress and Dissociation

Secondary traumatic stress, also known as vicarious trauma, is one step below suffering from post-traumatic stress disorder. While PTSD is triggered by direct/indirect exposure to trauma, secondary traumatic stress is a repercussion of caring for others in emotional pain. Listening to the trauma of childhood sexual abuse survivors can shift the view of a caregiver, resulting in negative beliefs and feelings about themselves and others. William Steele explains in *Reducing Compassion Fatigue, Secondary Traumatic Stress and Burnout: A Trauma-Sensitive Workbook* that when experiencing secondary trauma:

- We experience a state of ongoing hypervigilance for the next trauma or intense stress-inducing situation we might face.

- Our view of who and what is safe in our home and/or work environment changes.

- We feel a loss of power over our physiological and/or emotional responses when triggered by reminders of that stressful experience.

- As we experience feelings not felt before or not felt with such intensity, we come to feel unsafe with our emotions.

- We worry that our feelings will "leak" out, that others will discover that we are not managing as well as we say we are doing and question our competency.

- We do not feel as emotionally safe among our colleagues.

- We fear how they'll think of us if they discover the stress we are experiencing.

- We pull back from them, avoid them when we can, isolate ourselves more often.

- We do our best to avoid clients who intensify that stress.

- If we can't avoid them, we stop listening, try to redirect their focus or not return their calls in a timely manner.

- We start wondering if we will be able to continue to do what we do.

- We feel powerless to change anything.

- We're not driven by reason and logic any longer but by what we sense will make for even more stress.

- Reason and logic take a back seat to rationalizations. These rationalizations are stress-driven reactions and often create more problems for us—for example, how we interact with clients, the quality of our work, our performance.

- We no longer do what is logical and reasonable, but what we now sense we need to do to protect ourselves, to hold onto what sense of power we may have left.

Secondary traumatic stress may or may not coexist with compassion fatigue and burnout. Secondary traumatic stress has the ability to transform caregivers into the worse versions of themselves through **dissociation** in the same manner as Diana in Green Lantern's *The Blackest Night.*

Wonder Woman, the Blackest Night, and Secondary Traumatic Stress

Secondary traumatic stress has many of the same defining characteristics as post-traumatic stress disorder. This means that caregivers who suffer from secondary traumatic stress have trauma responses that are similar to the coping mechanisms of survivors. It is because caregivers can suffer from burnout, compassion fatigue, and secondary traumatic stress at the same time that they can become hypersensitive, angry, and irritable. All of the effects of caregiver fatigue transform caregivers into someone they do not recognize. They feel hijacked by their emotions and thoughts, no longer feeling like themselves as they battle **dissociation**.

Dissociation for a caregiver can best be described as operating on autopilot. Those who dissociate are not aware of actions or words after becoming unhinged mentally and/or physically due to the impact of secondary traumatic stress. Caregivers suffering from secondary traumatic stress attempt to block out their emotions and thoughts in an attempt to not become overwhelmed by their emotions and remain hypervigilant in the ability to appear professional, in control, and having it all together. Embodying the trauma exposure response of dissociation as a result of secondary traumatic stress causes caregivers to view themselves through the lens and pressure society places on them to behave in the manner of selfless superheroes, capable of enduring the mental hardships others cannot.

However, you, as a caregiver, are not a superhero. You are a human being with the same emotions as everyone else. This means that in order to retain balance and not suffer from secondary traumatic stress, caregivers must feel and process all of their emotions rather than prevent themselves from feeling the emotions that have been labeled as "weak" for professional caregivers. This is easier said than done.

Battling secondary traumatic stress requires processing and metabolizing the stress of listening to the trauma of others in a way that allows it to move through caregivers like a filter, rather than collecting in them like a cup always on the brink of running over. Caregivers who are unable to metabolize their trauma begin to suffer secondary traumatic stress and behave in a manner similar to that of a villain. These caregivers are unable to identify what needs to be done to alleviate their secondary traumatic stress to regain the balance needed to remain compassionate when helping survivors of trauma.

Author, Greg Rucka offers an excellent example of what it means to dissociate while suffering from secondary traumatic stress in *Wonder Woman: The Blackest Night* (2009) when Diana becomes possessed by a Black Lantern power ring. In the DC Comics epic event, the Green Lantern Corps (an intergalactic police force that uses emerald rings powered by the will and courage of its user to create mental constructs capable of battling evil and bringing justice to the universe) battles to stop the reanimation of the dead and the murder of the living by the Black Lantern Corps. The Green Lantern Corps works with different colored power rings on the emotional spectrum to prevent the destruction of the universe.

In *The Blackest Night*, Wonder Woman becomes possessed by a Black Lantern power ring, transforming into a perverted version of herself. Black Lantern power rings usually only reanimate the dead into evil zombies who feed on the emotions of others. However, because Diana died and was brought back to life, the ring is capable of taking possession of her body, controlling her actions and forcing her to hunt, hurt, and kill the people she loves. To depict Wonder Woman's loss of love and humanity, Diana's body and costume has lost its vibrant colors. No longer is her skin olive-toned and her costume red, gold, brown, and blue. Instead, she is a pale puppet washed of all color and spewing words of hatred. She no longer attempts to calm her adversary with words of hope and compassion, but instead continues to engage in battle.

As Wonder Woman attempts to kill her friend Mera, she either wears a smirk of contempt or a grimace of rage. While punching, beating, and taunting the queen of Atlantis, Diana says, "Everything, everyone you loved is dead! Atlantis dead! Arthur dead! Your son? Dead! So you'll forgive me, your highness, queen of the dead."

While Diana's body did and said things she did not believe to be true, she battled inside her own mind, telling herself, "Please, Athena, stop me from doing th— Don't make me do . . . I can't— I . . . I can't . . . can't . . . fight," and "Please, this isn't me—don't make me do this. Please, I beg you, don't make me do this."

Later, Diana is able to battle the effects of the Black Lantern ring and begins to regain some control over her actions, but not fully. Her skin remains black and white, and the black ring refuses to leave her body, but she prevents herself from killing Mera. As she battles the influence of the black ring, she imagines herself killing her friends Cassie Sandsmark, Donna Troy, and even her mother, Queen Hippolyta, before transforming back into her former self. On the outside, the Black Lantern Wonder Woman was filled with rage, cynicism, numbing, and compassion fatigue, while Diana internally battled the effects of burnout and guilt. She also suffered hallucinations of hurting the people she loves as she battled to regain control.

As a caregiver for trauma survivors, you may react to secondary traumatic stress in the same way Diana battles the Black Lantern power ring. Similar to Wonder Woman, you may feel trapped inside your own thoughts as a dissociation from reality, becoming unable to suppress feelings of anger, guilt, numbing, and cynicism. Unfortunately, without knowing and implementing strategies to manage the stress of helping survivors manage the trauma of their childhood sexual abuse, you continue to be the villain of your own story. The only way to battle secondary traumatic stress is to no longer live life by experiencing the sadness of the abyss followed by the joy of an Apotheosis. Instead, balance must be maintained through the use of trauma stewardship. The only way this can be achieved is by entering the Belly of the Whale and making the choice to begin the process of maintaining trauma stewardship.

Chapter Ten
Consequences of Not Maintaining
Trauma Stewardship
(Autobiographical)

"Those that started this war . . . they claimed to be doing it in the name of the mission of the Amazons. But you don't start a war to try and end a war. Violence begets violence. Unless someone breaks the cycle. That's usually me."

—**Wonder Woman**, *Justice League #49*, "The Darkseid War: Part 9" (2016)

In the midst of the 2020 COVID-19 pandemic, nurses, doctors, surgeons, and others working in the healthcare profession throughout the United States have been labeled as heroes by the news media. Commercials depict these individuals in scrubs and facemasks being applauded for their service with expressions of gratitude and accomplishment. However, what is not documented in the commercials and advertisements of honor driven servants is the burnout experienced by these healthcare workers after working twelve-hour shifts multiple days of the week, the compassion fatigue experienced from working with the severely sick, and the effects of secondary traumatic stress from having to make difficult decisions such as of who receives a ventilator and who should not due to the high probability that some are more likely than others to make it through the night. This grandiose view of healthcare workers can have detrimental psychological, social, and sometimes physical side effects.

It is true that these healthcare workers deserve recognition for the work they do day in and day out while battling this deadly virus that has claimed so many lives. These individuals have placed themselves and their families at risk by treating patients who are and may be infected with the coronavirus. What is not helpful is how these individuals are viewed by most of the public as selfless servants for those of us trapped in our homes, waiting for the all clear to resume our daily lives.

Experiencing the effects of a trauma exposure response, compounded by societal views of healthcare workers as selfless servants to the public, can make these workers feel like imposters rather than the heroes they are believed to be. This may be because of a belief that if they were truly heroes they would not feel so exhausted, sad, frustrated, depressed, or angry. They would feel happy to be of service to others and grateful that they have a job while so many others have been rendered unemployed, rather than bone-tired and depressed at having to work another twelve-hour shift. They believe that they should be able to take the heat and help those in need with a smile on their face and pep in their step.

It is because of these beliefs that they may also believe that asking for help in dealing with these emotions is a luxury they cannot afford when so many are suffering and counting on them to save the lives of those who view them as real-life superheroes. The grandiose view of their job pushes them to ignore their emotions and set aside the needs of their family for the greater good. Unfortunately, this view of caregivers as superheroes capable of enduring the impossible, rather than as individuals with their own needs, fears, emotions, and limitations, has not only psychological consequences, but physical consequences as well.

As a caregiver for survivors of childhood sexual abuse, you may experience the same grandiose thoughts or imposter's syndrome as the healthcare workers of COVID-19. These same psychological and physical side effects may also be a result of neglecting trauma stewardship. While I am not a healthcare worker or professional caregiver, I have come to understand the side effects of developing a trauma exposure response as childhood trauma survivor and public educator after experiencing the negative effects of the vagus nerve and developing a viral heart infection due to the buildup of unmanaged stress. It is for these reasons that I know there are consequences that extend beyond irritability, depression, anxiety, and earlier-than-expected grey hairs if trauma exposure response is not managed. While continuous suppression of trauma and chronic stress can sometimes fool you and those closest to you into believing everything is fine, the impact of compounding stress cannot be ignored by your body or the childhood sexual abuse survivors you serve who have experienced C-PTSD.

The Vagus Nerve and Withdrawing from College

In the fall of 2003, after only one week on campus, I withdrew from classes at Bowling Green State University in Ohio. This was partially due to my childhood sexual abuse, but at the time it was mostly because of not confronting the reality of being homeless with my mother throughout my junior and senior years in high school.

On paper, I was enrolled as a freshman at BGSU with free tuition and waived out-of-state fees after being awarded a scholarship for historically underrepresented minorities. Books, room, and board was all that needed to be paid out of pocket. Fortunately, after applying and earning numerous academic scholarships my senior year at Peoria High School in Illinois, these expenses were paid for as well. I should have been happy and eager to begin a new chapter in my life, and I was. It is for this reason the university was very confused about why I suddenly lost interest in being enrolled throughout the 2003 fall semester while also suffering an unexplainable gut-wrenching physical reaction that left me unable to get out of bed. The truth is, I *wanted* to stay. Attending college seemed to be my only option for survival and escape from a horrendous living situation.

Throughout my junior and senior years in high school, the moment of being on my own to make my own decisions free from the impact of my family was my primary source of motivation. The belief that one day I would be free from living in the basements of cousins, aunts, and uncles is what motivated my academic and extra-curricular activities while maintaining a part-time job delivering newspapers for the *Peoria Journal Star* each morning and setting up chairs for rehearsals and concerts for the Peoria Symphony Orchestra on evenings and weekends. Living a life free of the poor decisions of those who left me homeless with my mother and allowed me to be raped between the ages of eight and ten is what drove me to wake up each morning at four o'clock from fifth grade through senior year. It was the only way to ensure I had the funds needed for food, clothes, school supplies, gas, graduation fees, college application fees, and ACT testing. It is what drove me to enroll in classes on the honors track, studying late into the night in hopes of getting the opportunity that would allow me to attend college to better my living condition. It is the thought I latched onto when depression left me feeling hollow and numb to my own feelings and interactions with others. It was my belief that after achieving my goal, my life would be fixed and so I would be fixed. Unfortunately, I was wrong.

Immediately after unpacking my belongings and watching as my mother drove away to return to Illinois, a knot developed in my stomach that would not go away. No matter what I ate, watched on television, or thought about gave me the strength needed to rise from bed to attend class or finish the weekly readings. The sensation was like nothing I had ever experienced, and not one I would inflict on my worst enemy. The pains and their accompanying thoughts left me in uncontrollable tears, confused about what was happening to me and why. Now, after years of therapy and researching the effects trauma and chronic stress can have on the body, I know that the agitation of the vagus nerve was the source of my torment.

When an individual is severely in distress or feeling threatened, the vagus nerve becomes activated. This nerve runs from the base of the skull, through the body, and comes to an end at the colon. When threatened, the vagus nerve dries out the throat, increases the heart rate, causes gut-wrenching pain, and speeds up or slows down an individual's breathing, depending on the circumstances of the threat. Because I had ignored the complex trauma of being sexually abused as a child, lived with the chronic stress of an unstable household throughout all of my young adult life, and lived in the basement of relatives for two years while attempting to excel in academic and extra-curriculars in hopes of escaping to college, my fight-flight-or-freeze response kicked into overdrive, forcing the vagus nerve to cause gut-wrenching pains in my stomach. Within a week, this physical pain and sinking depression caused me to withdraw from classes at Bowling Green and forfeit all of the scholarships I had worked tirelessly to earn while in high school. Luckily, the university gave me a year to return (which I did) without having to reapply for admission, but with no reassurance that my historically underrepresented scholarship would be available the following fall (which it was).

By maintaining the illusion of having it all together and being in control, I was able to fool my friends, family, teachers, coaches, counselors, and myself that everything was fine, but it could not fool my body. The impact of bottling in my emotions rather than expressing my sadness, anger, frustration, and fear of the unknown resulted in a physical reaction that left me incapacitated and unable to fulfill my dream of attending college on the timetable I had set for my life. Later, after continuing to ignore the feeling of burnout due to a stress-filled work environment in Baltimore City, I was left with a viral heart infection and questions of my own mortality.

Viral Heart Infections and Maintaining the Illusion

In the late winter of 2017, while sitting at my desk grading papers in Baltimore City, my heart rate began to accelerate unexpectedly. At the time, I became only slightly alarmed, believing it to be another panic attack that could be easily managed by performing a few quick breathing exercises learned while in therapy. However, my anxiety dramatically increased, transforming my sense of control into unmanageable fear, when my left arm went numb and the pain in my chest became overwhelming. Concerned when the pain would not vanish after a few minutes of practiced breathing, I visited the school nurse, who took my blood pressure, saw that it was exceptionally high, and called an ambulance against my wishes to return to my classroom and finish the day teaching.

By the time the ambulance arrived, the pain in my chest had become so exhausting that I found it difficult to lift my left arm, which lay limp at my side. Once in the hospital, the doctors believed that, because of my age and good health, I had experienced a false alarm and would be free to go when the results of my blood work revealed as such. Unfortunately, when the results returned, it was evident that I had suffered some sort of cardiac event they could not explain, but it had put enough strain on my heart to release chemicals identifying the strain into my bloodstream. This meant keeping me overnight to keep track of my vitals and wait for my blood levels to return to normal. After being released, I was given instructions to follow up with a cardiac specialist and not return to work until I had done so.

Over the next few days as I waited for the scheduled appointment with my specialist, the pain in my chest settled to a consistent dull ache, and the weakness in my left arm was so severe it was placed in a sling to reduce its pain. When the day of my appointment arrived, the specialist asked if I'd had any previous heart problems, and my thoughts returned to two incidents in high school and college.

In 2003, during the track season my senior year, a pain began to develop in my chest any time I ran more than a lap. Considering I was used to running five to seven miles at a time, this was major. The pain then was not as crippling as the chest pain in 2017, but it was persistent and forced me to end my season sooner than expected. I never went to the hospital because at the time my mom and I could not afford the health bills, since the foreclosure of our home forced us to live in the basement of a relative's home. I also did not care for track, so I wasn't that broken up about having to cut my season short. Cross country was always more of my jam. Honestly, who wants to *watch* someone run in circles for two miles, let alone actually *run* in circles for two miles?

Later, in college, the pain returned. Rather than occurring while running, the pain in my chest was a dull ache that persisted for multiple days and severe enough to force me to visit the Wood County Hospital Emergency Room. While there, nurses hooked me up to an EKG machine, found nothing, and said I had an enlarged heart that was bruising the inside of my chest cavity. Without running any further tests, the doctor told me to take ibuprofen and eventually the pain would dissipate. There is no record of this visit, because at the time I did not have health insurance, and even if I had, the paperwork would have probably been lost, considering Wood County Hospital was known by the locals as being only slightly better than a death trap.

Hearing all of this confused the specialist, causing her to question how any doctor was capable of diagnosing an enlarged heart without performing an echocardiogram. Performing an echocardiogram of her own, she was able to determine that I did not have an enlarged heart, but I did have pericarditis, a viral heart infection in which the pericardial sac surrounding the heart and helps keep it in place becomes infected. It is an infection that affects one in every eighty thousand people a year, for reasons that are unknown. The only known way to heal from pericarditis is with rest and ibuprofen. If the infection becomes chronic, the pericardial sac must be removed.

Needless to say, I was concerned, but I was also surprised and confused. If pericarditis infects so few people every year, how did I get it three times in my lifetime? The doctor could not explain it, or that it was even true, due to the lack of medical records. To help in answering some of these questions, I went through a battery of tests to understand what was happening to my heart. Each chest x-ray, MRI, and echocardiograph came back inconclusive, leading to the same belief that I was suffering from a viral heart infection. To this day, I still have chest pains that result in more tests to ensure my heart is healthy, which leads to the question of why I have suffered from a viral heart infection multiple times in my life, considering I eat healthy, drink moderately, and exercise daily. The answer is burnout and chronic stress.

While in high school, I battled depression in an inescapable living condition while attempting to maintain the illusion of having it all together. Each morning I woke up filled with fear of what the day would bring, and I went to sleep exhausted from suppressing my true emotions with a smile that fooled those closest to me into believing everything was okay. College was the same as high school. The stress of living without the comfort of a safety net of family to catch me if I made a mistake financially, on top of competing most weekends on the BGSU Forensics Speech and Debate Team, working part-time at the Kohl Hall front desk, and maintaining the needed GPA to remain eligible for my academic scholarship, made living exhausting from its unpredictability. However, the incident in 2017 that put me in the hospital due to a viral heart infection was different than the stress-filled incidents in high school and college. This was due to burnout and a form of revictimization.

At the time, I was teaching seventh-grade humanities in Baltimore City and had recently published my memoir, *Raped Black Male*. Following its publication, some of my students wished to read it, so I placed a few in my classroom library. My students knew I had written the book because, similar to all my previously published books, I used it as an example to show my students the complexity of the publication process, but that it could be accomplished if they wanted to publish their own book one day. Unfortunately, when my principal saw a few of my students reading my memoir, she called me into her office.

While there, I was told that if students wished to read my memoir, they would need a signed permission slip from a parent or guardian, the books that were already in student's possession needed to be collected immediately, and that I was not allowed to say I was a survivor of childhood sexual abuse while on school grounds. After leaving her office, for reasons I could not explain at the time, I felt afraid.

I collected the distributed memoirs from my students, told them they had to have a signed permission slip to continue reading (which some of them brought in), and left for the day feeling anxious and on edge. At the time, I did not understand the cause of my discomfort, but I do now. After years of being forced to remain silent about my sexual assault as a male survivor, to be told to remain silent about my victimization by another authoritative female figure was like being victimized for a second time.

From that moment on, I felt burned out from working in an oppressive work environment. I no longer felt happy about going into work. The dread I used to feel at the beginning of my career as an educator had returned, making walking out the door in the morning difficult, but not impossible because of learned relaxation techniques, medication, and therapy. While at work, I was filled with fear, terrified of being called back into my principal's office to be reprimanded for a second time. Checking my email and feeling the vibration of my phone filled me with an overwhelming sense of anxiety. Susan, my therapist, said I needed to quit, but how could I? I needed to provide for my family.

Finally, after taking a personal day to speak at a local high school about what it means to be a male survivor, and being texted by my principal that she was to be informed of days requested off regardless of whether or not the proper paperwork was completed and turned in, I told her that she was filling me with an overwhelming fear of coming to work and doing my job. When I returned to school, we had another conference; this time the vice principal was in attendance. Rather than apologize for making me feel uncomfortable as a professional, she doubled down on her order that I not state I was a survivor of childhood sexual abuse while on school grounds. It was shortly afterward the viral heart infection occurred.

These incidents throughout my life help me understand the truth of Bessel Van der Kolk's book *The Body Keeps the Score*. An individual may be capable of fighting the feelings brought on due to trauma and chronic stress. In fact, they may even be able to forget they ever occurred. Although this may be true, the body does not forget. If stress and trauma are not processed, they have the ability to catch up to the mind and body, causing detrimental (sometimes irreversible) effects. It is for this reason that trauma stewardships are vital for the wellbeing of caregivers. It ensures they do all they can to metabolize the stress and trauma accumulated in the body from helping others heal. If trauma stewardship cannot be maintained due to burnout because of an unhealthy work environment, it may be best to leave, start a new job, and protect the safety of your mental health.

Part Four
Saving Your Inner Wonder Woman: Achieving Balance and Completing the Caregiver's Journey of Healing

"There is far more to the human spirit than war. Though war is always there, there is also passion, and hope, and truth."

—**Wonder Woman**, *Justice League #32*, "Justice / Doom War, Part 3" (2019)

Practicing trauma stewardship does not mean taking on more responsibilities in an attempt to fight through the pain. The only answer is to let go of beliefs of grandiosity. Harboring thoughts that the only way out of pain is by working through it only strengthens and accelerates the trauma exposure responses of burnout, compassion fatigue, and secondary traumatic stress. This is a lesson Diana learns the hard way in 2016's *Wonder Woman Volume #7,* "War-Torn."

In "War-Torn," Diana attempts to juggle the responsibilities of being Wonder Woman, a member of the Justice League, queen of the Amazons, and the god of war. She believes she can do it all in an attempt to numb and suppress the pain associated with being the god of war. Over coffee, Hessia, an exiled Amazon and Diana's friend, warns:

> *You've become the physical personification of violence, bloodshed, and death. You are war now. You need to prepare yourself so that you can shape the god you'll become . . . because if you're not careful, it'll shape you. You'll become Ares, violent and dangerous. Ares used alcohol to numb the pain of who he was. What lengths will you go to in order to make the pain stop? And how will your friends in the Justice League respond when you do?*

Hessia's warning to Diana is not only true for Wonder Woman, but for caregivers as well. What lengths will you go to in order to numb the trauma exposure response after assimilating some of the pain of survivors you are trying to help heal? Will you drink to numb the anger, or dissociate to no longer speak the words of a cynic?

Diana takes on the trauma exposure response of workaholism. Her attention is pulled in so many different directions that she does not notice a coup rising against her, resulting in the death of her Amazon brothers who were discarded by their mothers and sold to Hephaestus for weapons. Her lack of balance results in a way of life she is unable to maintain, and tears of blood run from her eyes as she suppresses her anger and rage. As a caregiver, the suppression of emotions will not result in blood running from your eyes, but it will result in burnout, compassion fatigue, and secondary trauma stress. The only answer to this problem is learning to practice trauma stewardship.

This part of the guide does not discuss how to practice self-care through meditation, mindfulness, and yoga. Although these have been proven to help relieve stress, they can lose their effectiveness for caregivers due to time constraints and pressure to maintain a schedule that only creates more stress. This final part of the guide helps caregivers make the decision to practice trauma stewardship by entering the **Belly of the Whale**, identifying the causes of compassion fatigue and secondary trauma stress when **Crossing the First Threshold**, learning from past mistakes to become better individuals and caregivers through **Atonement**, and maintaining balance when becoming the **Master of Two Worlds**.

Chapter Eleven
Entering the Belly of the Whale

"I chose to come among you, to learn and to teach. To bring our worlds closer together."

—**Diana Prince**, *Wonder Woman: Earth One, Volume Two* (2018)

Wonder Woman is not a perfect superhero. In fact, she has gone so far as committing murder for the greater good. In *Wonder Woman (Volume 2) #219*, "Sacrifice, Part IV" (2005), Wonder Woman snaps the neck of villain Maxwell Lord while he's wrapped in her golden lasso of truth. At the time, she believes it is the only way to ensure Lord is no longer capable of using his mind-controlling abilities to harness the destructive powers of Superman. Unfortunately, her actions are not able to be swept under the rug. Somehow, footage of Lord's murder is leaked, causing the public to lose faith in the heroes they once blindly trusted.

Maxwell's Lord's manipulative actions while alive, and the death at her hands, forces Diana to change her view of the world and her role as Wonder Woman. She begins to lose her way as the Amazon ambassador of peace.

In *Infinite Crisis* (2006), while arguing with Superman and Batman regarding her decision to kill Lord, she minimizes her actions, thinks in absolute terms, and aggrandizes her role as Wonder Woman when she says, "I told you the world doesn't need Diana. The world needs Wonder Woman. That maniac murdered Ted Kord. And he was going to use you to do the same to Bruce. There was no choice."

Luckily, Diana comes to realize that she is not perfect and her actions are flawed. However, rather than hold herself accountable and take the necessary steps to move forward, she views herself as a failure.

After being given the opportunity to speak to an elder version of herself from a different Earth, Diana believes her doppelganger has arrived to announce her failure as an ambassador of peace. However, this is not the case. Instead of telling Diana she is a failure, the Wonder Woman of Earth Two tells the Amazon princess that her mission has come to an end and she can stop attempting to be perfect. She tells Diana, "You've been a princess, a goddess, an ambassador, and a warrior. But the one thing you haven't been for a very long time is human. Despite all of the flaws within humanity, there are just as many strengths. Remember . . . everyone makes mistakes."

Wonder Woman's words of wisdom are not only beneficial to Diana's forgiveness of herself and her past actions, but for caregivers as well as they begin their journey of healing. Grandiosity only leads to trauma exposure responses of burnout, compassion fatigue, and secondary traumatic stress. To begin the process of changing these views means acknowledging that you as a caregiver are human, capable of developing a trauma exposure response. And, like any human, you have feelings, make mistakes, and are not perfect. Accepting this means entering the **Belly of the Whale,** making the difficult decision to acknowledge your trauma exposure response and beginning the process of practicing trauma stewardship.

The Belly of the Whale

Joseph Campbell describes the belly of the whale in *Hero with a Thousand Faces* as the point in a hero's journey when they are willing to undergo the change needed to transform from the person they were into the hero they could become. Although similar, entering the Belly of the Whale during the healing journey of a caregiver is slightly different. When a professional caregiver or loved one of a survivor of childhood sexual abuse enter the Belly of the Whale, they are not striving to become a hero. Instead, they are making the choice to begin the process of bringing balance to their lives by practicing trauma stewardship. This means having the courage to admit they are not perfect, foregoing their grandiose beliefs of their profession or actions as a caregiver. It also means having the willingness to put in the effort to recognize their trauma exposure responses. It is about the willingness to accept that helping others means being willing to recognize your flaws as a caregiver and lean on others for support.

Wonder Woman, Cheetah, Hera, and Facing the Truth

When entering the Belly of the Whale, professional caregivers must make the choice to see the truth about themselves and their profession rather than remain blind to the harmful side effects of guiding trauma survivors through the process of healing. This is the only way to combat burnout and compassion fatigue. Diana helps to demonstrate how this can be done when battling Cheetah and choosing to follow her own path as Wonder Woman rather than the grandiose views and selfish objectives of her patrons.

In 2019's *Wonder Woman #82*, "The Wild Hunt: Part 1," Diana wonders who she is as Wonder Woman without her Bracelets of Submission and the Golden Perfect. As mentioned in Chapter Eight, Wonder Woman was defeated by Cheetah following the death of Aphrodite, the Greek goddess of love. While wearing Diana's crown, wielding the Golden Perfect, and brandishing God Killer, Cheetah ravages Themyscira, imprisoning Amazons. Cheetah is doing this in hopes of drawing the attention of the queen of the gods, Hera. It is her belief that if she kills the gods, Diana will be free from their domineering control. Although misguided, Cheetah is doing this in the hopes that she can help Diana reach her full potential and repay the debt owed to Wonder Woman for freeing her from the control of the god, Urzkartaga.

In *Wonder Woman #750*, "The Wild Hunt: Finale" (2020), Diana is forced to face the truth about herself, Cheetah, and her connection to the Greek gods as their champion. Without her crown, Bracelets of Submission, or lasso of truth, Diana realizes that neither Cheetah nor Hera are wrong or right. She explains to the vigilante, Honor, as the villain and god battle one another:

> *Cheetah's crimes cannot be denied. Standing with the Legion of Doom. The murder of Aphrodite. She is lost. She threatens my fellow Amazons and the very gods we champion. All in my name, to repay some imagined debt she's been manipulated into seeing. She lashes out, despite my constant efforts. So much has been lost. I lost Steve Trevor. And as I battled the Legion of Doom, he lost A.R.G.U.S. His life's work, and I wasn't there. I am angry, Honor. More than in a long time. But Cheetah wanted this. She's made herself my enemy. And I, even now, despite all she's done, I must find the strength to care. Now, more than ever, at my darkest, I must remember her.*

Diana's words ring true for professional caregivers who are burned out or suffering compassion fatigue. Similar to Diana, caregivers can become angry. They can become angry at the system that sometimes disenfranchises the survivors they work selflessly to help heal. They can be angry at the rules and regulations of their own profession for putting too much pressure to succeed without supplying adequate resources to meet the high level of success. They can become angry at themselves for losing the spark they once possessed due to the development of a trauma exposure response. Finally, they can become angry at the survivors they seek to help heal when they suffer setbacks in their recovery due to avoidance and cognitive distortions created by their C-PTSD.

However, like Diana, caregivers must use the wisdom they have accumulated, and draw from the strength of other caregivers exhibiting compassion who are willing to lend a helping hand when available. Diana does this when she uses the Golden Perfect to bind herself, Hera, and Cheetah in its truth-revealing abilities. Doing this allows her to see the truth in herself, her superiors, and those she seeks to help reform.

Confronting Yourself

First, Diana faces herself in the same way caregivers must face their own thoughts and actions, leading to their burnout, compassion fatigue, and then entering the Belly of the Whale. Diana tells Cheetah and Hera, "And I have struggles of late. Love and truth have been . . . challenging to find. So where better than to address that with two who have so strongly influenced me. Hera, you inspired my mission of peace. You also stood in its way when it suited you."

Diana notices that love, truth, and compassion have stood in the way of her mission of peace. Caregivers must do the same. They must reflect on their own actions and hold themselves accountable for not taking the time needed to remain in balance. Afterward, Diana regains possession of the Golden Perfect and a piece of herself she believed was lost. Caregivers who do the same regain a sense of understanding themselves and the motivations behind their actions.

Confronting Those Who Have Been Victimized

Next, Diana confronts Cheetah in the same way caregivers must approach helping those who have been victimized as children in a manner that is stern but compassionate. Binding Cheetah with the Golden Perfect in a way that would slice the neck of the villain if she resisted its truth, Diana tells Cheetah:

> I understand what you're doing for me. And there may be wisdom in your goals. But you cannot ignore the truth you saw in the lasso. You haven't listened to what I want. You've become

what you hate most. Like our patrons, you claim knowledge and assistance. When in truth, you lord over our own choices. Ignore us. Don't you see? In your righteous fury to free me from the gods, you've all but become one, Barbara Ann.

Afterward, Diane offers to help her friend begin the process of healing. Unfortunately, she refuses, running off into the night once freed from the lasso. Diana does not pursue her former friend. She lets her go. Loved ones of trauma survivors must be willing to have the same level of compassion for those they seek to help heal from their childhood sexual abuse. Similar to Diana, caregivers and loved ones must have the courage to speak the truth to survivors when they practice avoidance, exhibit cognitive distortions, or practice unhealthy coping mechanisms such as self-harm, drugs, alcohol, or other addictions. This is not done out of a place of hatred, but honesty. It is the only way to help those who have been victimized to view their thoughts and actions through the lens of a survivor rather than a victim. This is the only way to not only help survivors heal, but reduce the effects of compassion fatigue on caregivers, helping caregivers regain their crown in the same manner as Wonder Woman after she revealed the truth to Barbara Ann. If individuals who have been victimized choose not to heal and hurt you in the process, you must also have the courage to allow the survivor the opportunity to continue their journey without you by their side.

Confronting Administrators

Finally, Diana confronts Hera in the same manner that professional caregivers must face the possibility of perpetuated toxic behaviors and practices of administrators in their workplace. Kneeling on one knee, Diana tells Hera:

I think, in a way ... Cheetah was right. Thank you, to you and all my patrons. You've inspired me, given me strength and direction. But my recent setbacks, losing some of those closest to me . . . this chaos that's become my life has shown me I need to refocus. To redefine. My mission must continue, but not under your guidance, or anyone else's. The mission of Wonder Woman must be defined by Wonder Woman. I've been pulled in too many directions. When my true compass should be my heart alone. Thank you, Hera. Again. Always. But I do not need you anymore.

Diana's words prove she is worthy of being called Truth Queen. Here, Diana recognizes the help and guidance offered by her patrons, but she knows that if she is going to be able to continue as Wonder Woman, she must forge her own path. Caregivers must be willing to make the same hard truth if they are going to prevent burnout and administrators are unwilling or incapable of change. Reaching these conclusions about yourself as a caregiver, those you seek to help heal, and those who direct you on your path of professionalism, is the only way to enter the Belly of the Whale and begin practicing trauma stewardship.

First Steps Toward Entering and Exiting the Belly of the Whale

After making the decision to practice trauma stewardship and enter the Belly of the Whale, it is important to understand that it can be easier to heal from compassion fatigue than burnout. This is because of the long-standing cultural norms in the workplace and ingrained beliefs and practices in the profession of being a professional caregiver. Although this may be true, there are tests that can be taken to indicate if an individual is suffering from the effects of burnout.

In *Overcoming Compassion Fatigue: A Practical Resilience Workbook* (2014), authors Martha Teater and John Ludgate asks caregivers to consider these signs of stress and how they impact them personally. When writing your responses, it may be helpful to keep track of the answers to these questions in a personal notebook or journal.

Psychological Signs

- I am easily frustrated, irritable, or annoyed.
- I tend to isolate myself and avoid people.
- There are times that I feel more sadness than the situation calls for.
- Sometimes I feel inadequate or ineffective.
- My attitude has become more negative.
- I have intrusive thoughts or images of someone else's suffering or trauma.
- I have become preoccupied with the suffering of others.
- There are times that I have difficulty feeling tender, warm, intimate emotions.
- I have felt detached or different from other people.
- I have felt anger at the perpetrator or casual event of someone's pain.
- I have experienced vague feelings of guilt.
- There are times when I feel a loss of personal safety and control and more vulnerability to danger.
- Sometimes it appears that my work has hardened me to other people.
- There's been a change in my sense of humor; it's become darker and more cynical or sarcastic.
- I see myself in a more negative light.
- I've had some signs of depression (sadness, loss of interest in things I used to enjoy, social isolation, etc.).
- I'm less sensitive and empathetic than I used to be.
- I've been more resentful and angrier.
- I'm enjoying my work less.

Physical Signs

- I've had more physical concerns (headaches, stomach upset, more illnesses, high blood pressure, etc.).
- I get sorer and achier than I used to.
- My sleep habits have changed or I'm fatigued.
- My health isn't as good as it used to be.

Behavioral Signs

- I'm over-alert, restless, jumpy, nervous, or easily startled.
- I'm more hypervigilant or aware of my surroundings.
- I see a change in my response to violence; I'm numb or more sensitive to it.
- I've had difficulty thinking clearly or trouble making decisions.
- I'm using alcohol or other drugs more than usual.
- There is a change in my desire for intimacy, or my desire for sex is lower.
- I'm acting angrier and have a shorter fuse.
- I have an exaggerated sense of responsibility and feel too many things fall to me to do.
- I'm more forgetful.
- I've had difficulty with personal relationships and am not as easy to get along with as I used to be.

Signs at Work

- I feel overwhelmed by the needs of others around me.
- I'm less committed to my work.
- I've had some resentment toward my employer.
- I've missed work at times, or I've shown up late.
- My boundaries are different, either too rigid or too loose.

- My work life and personal life aren't very well separated.
- I'm becoming less compassionate and empathetic.

Along with *Overcoming Compassion Fatigue*, the Maslach Burnout Inventory (Maslach, Jackson & Leiter, 1996) describes three aspects of burnout.

1. Emotional exhaustion
2. Depersonalization
3. Reduced personal accomplishment

And the Burnout Measure (BM) developed by Pines and Aronson (1978) measures the following:

1. Physical exhaustion
2. Emotional exhaustion
3. Mental exhaustion

Both tools can be accessed online to measure burnout. B. Hudnall Stamm also provides a free professional quality of life scale at www.proqol.org.

If you find that you are suffering from burnout and believe the climate and culture of your workplace can be changed for the better, put in the effort to help foster change, allow the practice to grow, and let your coworkers know they can lean on one another in times of difficulty. Everyone, including administrators, should feel comfortable helping one another maintain balance in their life by battling burnout in an attempt to prevent compassion fatigue and secondary traumatic stress

Chapter Twelve
Crossing the First Threshold

"Take my grandmother, Alcippe, she was our queen. But when she no longer felt respected by our gods, she defied them, and left our island. You might think we'd be angry at her, but she acted from her heart, challenged tradition, challenged power. To me she's an inspiration."

—**Diana Prince**, *Wonder Woman #755*, "The Four Horsewomen: Part 1" (2020)

The Amazonian warriors began their existence as victims of domestic violence who were resurrected by Greek goddesses in hopes of allowing them the opportunity to live a better life. Unfortunately, they were again victimized and enslaved by the demigod Herakles. Once free, they secluded themselves from the world in hopes of remaining safe, but they forever wore the bracelets from their chains as a reminder of their past abuse.

As a race, the Amazons suffered systematic oppression from those they strived to save in patriarch's world. On Paradise Island, they perfected their culture and connection to nature while furthering their knowledge. Although safe, the Amazons lived with a sense of grandiosity on Themyscira. It is this sense of righteousness and systematic oppression that fueled their justification for hurting others who share the same gender as their former oppressors.

In *Wonder Woman: Volume #2*, "Guts," (2012), Hephaestus, the Greek god of fire, reveals to Diana the imperfection of the Amazons and their victimization of men. He explains how three times a century, the Amazons leave Paradise Island, seduce sailors out at sea, and have their way with them. Afterward, the men are killed and tossed overboard. They do this in hopes of becoming pregnant. Those who have daughters are raised as Amazons, while the boys are either thrown into the sea to drown or traded with Hephaestus for weapons. To amend these wrongs, Diana brought the abandoned Amazon boys who grew into men to Paradise Island. Unfortunately, rather than face the truth of their own victimization of men, the female Amazons killed their brothers, leaving only one survivor.

Hephaestus's story and the actions of the Amazons helps to demonstrate how organizations cannot be forced to change dated and ineffective practices that cause burnout. The ways of functioning may be ingrained into the culture of a community, preventing the implementation of trauma stewardship. However, if professional caregivers make a collective effort with administration and organizations designed to help survivors enter and exit the Belly of the Whale, they **Cross the First Threshold** to become stronger, in the same manner as the Amazons when Themyscira is reimagined and improved with the help of leading innovators throughout the world for the betterment of all of humanity.

In 2002's *Wonder Woman #177*, "Paradise Found," Wonder Woman convinces her patrons and her Amazon sisters to change their practice of remaining secluded from the world, in order to become a beacon of hope, peace, and education for the rest of the world. To redesign Themyscira, they get the help of architect Henri Claude Tibet, Harvard professor Julia Kapatelis, Martian J'on J'onzz, pilot and engineer Steve Trevor, and Amazon master designer Kaleeza Fased.

Once the new Themyscira is complete, they invite the leaders of the world to share their knowledge with one another. On the day of Themyscira's reveal to the world, while surrounded by the best minds and peacemakers of the world, Amazon Chancellor Philippus says:

> *Visitors of every gender and species will be welcomed here,*
> *to debate theories, to craft treaties, to create art and literature,*

to devise medicines, to craft technologies, and to worship without fear in the manner that they choose. A truly democratic society which will depend on this competition of ideas in a space that will be fiercely protected by the very best our race has to offer. As before, an Amazon will represent us in the outer world, set forth with the task of representing us and spreading our highest ideals. The notions of peaceful coexistence, of equality, of love and respect. This Amazon truly is the very best our nation has to offer. And she will once again wear as a part of her garb a golden coronet. A tiara, which, stripped of its royal significance now has a new meaning as a constant symbol of our nation, and of our hope and dreams. We know this ambassador of peace as the daughter of a queen, and dearest Diana . . . but more of you have come to call her, Wonder Woman!

Striving to create a culture that furthers the ideals of its contributors while striving to improve the mental health and well-being of caregivers, administrators, and survivors is what it means to grow stronger and Cross the First Threshold together in healing and with balance. It means having the courage to admit a system has become ineffective and strive to improve it for all parties involved in an attempt to create equity. This is what it means to Cross the First Threshold and feel the full spectrum of emotions needed to do the work of helping survivors of childhood trauma heal.

Crossing the First Threshold

In a caregiver's journey of healing, Crossing the First Threshold begins with the process of identifying, understanding, and healing from the effects of burnout, compassion fatigue, and secondary traumatic stress by feeling all emotions and not just those categorized as being pleasant. Similar to Joseph Campbell's *Hero of a Thousand Faces*, when the hero can no longer go back to the life they used to live knowing what they now know, caregivers can no longer return to business as usual after experiencing and understanding the psychological, physical, and behavioral effects of burnout, compassion fatigue, or secondary traumatic stress. This is because doing so would be catastrophic to their mental health. For caregivers, this means no longer numbing emotions that have been stigmatized as being negative, but instead experiencing, identifying, and understanding all their emotions in an attempt to process their effects on their mind, body, and behavior.

Diana demonstrates this in *Blackest Night: Wonder Woman* after fighting the effects of the Black Lantern power ring to become a Star Sapphire and eventually a White Lantern.

Black Lanterns, Star Sapphires, and Feeling the Full Spectrum of Emotions

The sense of hopelessness created by compassion fatigue can be detrimental to a caregiver's well-being, forcing them to numb their emotions in an attempt to regain control over their mind, body, and sense of accomplishment in the workplace. Unfortunately, the trauma exposure response of dissociation only leads to less balance and more secondary traumatic stress. The only way to combat the numbing effects caused by dissociation is by doing just the opposite and allowing the body to feel and process all emotions rather than just those that have been stigmatized as positive. Although this may be easier said than done, this means knowing you are human and no longer allowing the need to appear perfect and being in complete control to dictate your life. Diana exhibits this in the DC Comic event *Blackest Night* featuring Wonder Woman.

It is easy to become numb to the effects of trauma in an attempt to remain in control and safe. Diana helps to explain why in *Blackest Night: Wonder Woman*, "Part One: The Living" (2009), when she says:

> *I walk with death. I do not follow death. Nor do I lead. Rather, death is at my side, the uneasy, constant companion of any warrior. I would say the same of all of us who live. Death is*

the natural result of life . . . I accept death. I have learned to. I have lost many to its call. Far too many. I am an Amazon. I have had no choice. I have lived through death myself. I did not care for it. The demon Neron assaulted my soul, raked and burnt it. I lingered for days before finally dying. I speak with experience when I say that living is better, no matter how hard, no matter how painful.

Here, Wonder Woman explains how she has grown accustomed to death. As an Amazon, she has seen death and believes death no longer affects her the way it would others who have not walked with it at their side. In essence, she has become numb to its effects. However, for caregivers, it is not death they have grown numb to experiencing, but the pain associated with trauma. Caregivers believe, in the same manner as Wonder Woman, that they have walked with trauma. They do not follow trauma, nor do they lead. Rather, trauma is constantly at their side.

Unfortunately, because trauma is constantly at their side, they may have begun to grow numb to its effects while believing they retain the same sense of love and compassion Wonder Woman believes she has retained after walking with death for most of her life. Although Diana is capable of embodying love when faced with the evil of others such as Maxwell Lord, being capable of always embodying compassion as a caregiver when faced with the trauma of survivors of childhood sexual abuse is an impossibility. Eventually, the emotions will become too powerful, causing the caregiver to go numb like Diana after becoming possessed by a Black Lantern ring and eventually rage out of control in a similar manner as Mera when possessed by a Red Lantern ring in *Blackest Night: Wonder Woman,* "Part One: The Living."

Mera's Rage

The continued suppression of emotions that are perceived as negative is similar to the violent shaking of a bottled carbonated beverage. Shaking the bottled beverage causes the pressure to build inside. Although the carbonation is contained, the more the container is shaken, the more the pressure builds. If opened, intentionally or unintentionally, by someone who does not know the bottle has been shaken, the contents of the bottle fizz over and spray out of control, preventing the top from being replaced until the pressure has been released. Similarly, if emotions of sadness, depression, grief, and anxiety are continuously suppressed, eventually the emotions can no longer be contained, resulting in uncontrollable rage that is a result of secondary traumatic stress.

Mera, the wife of Arthur Curry (Aquaman) and queen of Atlantis, exhibits this rage when she comes into contact with and becomes a member of the Red Lantern Corps, which in *Blackest Night* represents rage on the emotional spectrum. The comic explains that because red is on the furthest edges of the emotional spectrum, Red Lanterns are unable to think clearly or be reasoned with. What makes them different from other Lantern Corps is that when an individual becomes a member of the Red Lantern Corps, their blood is replaced with a plasma that has the same qualities as napalm and sprayed through the mouth. Mera exhibits all of these characteristics of a Red Lantern at the same moment Wonder Woman becomes a Star Sapphire.

Diana is capable of overcoming the numbing effects caused from becoming a member of the Black Lantern Corps. Instead, she becomes a beacon of love and compassion when she becomes a Star Sapphire. However, when Mera becomes a member of the Red Lantern Corps, she did not become filled love and compassion. Instead, the rage she had been suppressing throughout much of her adult life was no longer able to be contained. Similar to the contents of the previously mentioned bottled carbonated beverage that has been shaken and opened, Mera's rage is expelled from her mouth in the form of napalm blood plasma. She does not speak, only blindly fights those standing in her way, friend or foe.

In *Blackest Night: Wonder Woman,* "Part Three: A Hint of Daylight," Diana encounters this shortly after becoming a Star Sapphire. She explains Mera's rage when she thinks to herself, "So much rage, it consumes her. Consumes reason. Consumes life. I can feel the ring sifting through the red haze. Searching memory and heartbreak. Searching in vain as her rage runs rampant. Rage fed by inconceivable pain, hidden behind years of lies."

Here, Mera is raging out of control due to the suppression of grief following the murder of her son, Arthur Curry Jr. (Aquababy), by villain Black Manta; mourning the unexpected death of her husband, Arthur Curry (Aquaman); and managing the stress that accompanies ruling Atlantis, the largest kingdom on Earth. Similar to Mera, professional caregivers may become filled with rage when attempting to suppress their frustration with the inadequacy of a system that is supposed to help childhood survivors of sexual trauma but sometimes causes more harm than good. Rather than become numb and burned out in the same manner as Wonder Woman after becoming a Black Lantern, these individuals develop the trauma exposure response of becoming filled with rage similar to Mera after becoming a Red Lantern. They do this in an attempt to battle their feelings of secondary traumatic stress that has consumed their being, leaving the caregiver with nothing left to give.

In the same manner that Mera can only calm her rage after being shown the truth of the source of her anger by Wonder Woman and the Golden Perfect, professional caregivers and loved ones of trauma survivors can only calm their rage when given the same opportunity to face the truth. A caregiver's job is not to suppress their rage or numb their emotions. Instead, they should attempt to understand why they are feeling angry by being honest with themselves about its source. Diana exhibits how to do this while battling Mera and thinking, "So much anger. Too much, Why? It's not just rage. It's more than that. It's a kind of hatred. And it runs deep. Deeper than my ring can reveal. Or at least can reveal alone."

Afterward, she wraps the Golden Perfect around Mera, experiencing the queen of Atlantis's pain and grief with her. To relieve secondary traumatic stress, caregivers must work with one another in an attempt to understand the emotions. In the same manner that survivors of childhood sexual abuse cannot heal without the help of others, caregivers cannot cross the first threshold without the help of others who acknowledge, validate, and do not judge their ability to have the courage to feel all their emotions in the same manner as the White Lantern Corp.

Becoming a White Lantern

As explained in chapter eight, when Wonder Woman becomes infected with the Black Lantern power ring, it is similar to the effects of a caregiver going numb due to burnout and compassion fatigue. And, as explained above, when Mera comes into possession of the Red Lantern power ring, it is similar to the effects of a caregiver being filled with rage from the effects of secondary traumatic stress.

Luckily, Diana was able to fight the effects of becoming a Black Lantern long enough to become a Star Sapphire, and Mera was able to understand the true source of her rage as a Red Lantern after becoming bound by the Golden Perfect. However, both Diana's love and Mera's rage are still too weak to defeat those who have become Black Lanterns in *Blackest Night*. It's true, both have the ability to stun Black Lanterns, but both need the help of other Lanterns on the emotional spectrum to severe the individual's connection to the Black Lantern ring. It is not until Diana and the other members of the Justice League become White Lanterns that this is possible.

The white light of the White Lantern Corps that is capable of defeating Black Lanterns can only be created by combining all colors on the emotional spectrum. As a caregiver, this demonstrates that love is not enough to defeat the effects of compassion fatigue and secondary traumatic stress. Instead, all emotions must be mobilized if a trauma exposure response is ever going to end.

Similar to Wonder Woman becoming a White Lantern, caregivers must harness all their emotions and understand them when Crossing the First Threshold. Caregivers must have the ability to be as brave as a Green Lantern to battle the effects of trauma alongside the survivors they strive to help heal, love those who sometimes cannot love themselves due to the effects of childhood trauma with the same intensity as a Star Sapphire, jealously guard their sense of self-worth and mental well-being with the same ferocity as an Orange Lantern, sense the fear of a Yellow Lantern when attempting to imagine a reality without the hope of Blue Lanterns, and know that it would not be possible without retaining the compassion of the Indigo Tribe for everyone, including themselves.

Feeling with the Entire Emotional Spectrum

Crossing the First Threshold means beginning the process of learning to feel and manage *all* emotions, rather than those that have been deemed acceptable and good throughout society. A way of accomplishing this task is with a **subjective unit of distress scale (SUDS)**.

The structure of the scale included in this portion of the guide uses the emotional spectrum of the nine different Lanterns throughout the DC universe to help caregivers develop the ability to read their own emotions in relation to experiencing burnout, compassion fatigue, and secondary traumatic stress.

What sets this SUDS scale apart from others is that it's designed to help caregivers maintain balance while practicing good trauma stewardship along their journey of healing. This SUDS scale is also different because the goal is for caregivers to not only have the ability to read and manage their emotions, but also to use to manage their emotions in a way that maintains balance throughout their professional and personal lives. This does not mean experiencing all the emotions on the spectrum at once. Instead, it means having the ability to understand emotions in a way that means understanding the emotion's location on the spectrum in relation to regaining, falling out of, or maintaining balance while practicing good trauma stewardship. Lingering too long on either end of the spectrum can lead to burnout, compassion fatigue, or secondary traumatic stress.

While it is important to experience all of these emotions, it is just as important to understand why and how to manage these emotions to maintain equilibrium. Even when experiencing emotions that are perceived to be positive, it is important to never allow one to overpower the others.

"THE BLACKEST NIGHT" EMOTIONAL SPECTRUM SUBJECTIVE UNITS OF DISTRESS SCALE			
Color on the Emotional Spectrum	**Emotion on the Spectrum**	**Name of Lantern**	**Description in Relation to Maintaining Balance**
White	Life	White Lantern Corps	In *Blackest Night,* the only way to sever the connection of a Black Lantern from its host is through the use of multiple Lanterns on the emotional spectrum working together. While White Lanterns do not exist on the emotional spectrum, they do represent the embodiment of life itself

			and the combination of emotions working together to achieve balance. This means that the goal of a caregiver attempting to practice trauma stewardship and maintain balance throughout their life is learning to achieve the equilibrium of emotions of a White Lantern and embody the will of life and balance itself throughout their actions. Experiencing only one emotion has the ability to tip the scales, leading to burnout and compassion fatigue. However, it is also important to remember that experiencing all emotions on the spectrum without understanding their origins or effects can become overwhelming, leading to secondary traumatic stress. This is not the goal. Instead, maintain equilibrium through continuous embodiment of the needed emotions to guide

			survivors along their path of healing while continuing along their own journey of self-care.
Green	Will	Green Lantern Corps	Green Lanterns are the most well known throughout the DC universe in the characters of Hal Jordan, John Stewart, and Kyle Rayner. Their will and courage to continue fighting against sometimes impossible odds is what drives the Green Lantern Corps toward facing their greatest fear. Similarly, caregivers must possess the will to fight and help survivors of trauma to heal. While only possessing will and courage will cause a caregiver to fall out of balance, the courage of will must accompany each listed emotion if equilibrium is going to be maintained. Without will as the driving motivation behind each interaction, burnout, compassion

			fatigue, and secondary traumatic stress become a serious possibility. It is the glue that binds the emotions together while supplying the need to continue moving forward.
Indigo	Compassion	Indigo Tribe	The source of the Indigo Tribe's power originates from having the willingness to understand the connection and motivations of others while also knowing and understanding everyone makes mistakes. Caregivers who believe they embody the traits of compassion possessed by the Indigo Tribe have the ability to understand their own motivations while not hating themselves for being human and making mistakes. These caregivers progress toward growth rather than perfection, allowing themselves and others to move along their journey

			at their own pace while. Caregivers who embody the emotion of compassion not only need the will that powers Green Lanterns, but also the love of the Star Sapphires. One without the others unbalances the equation of understanding and feeling emotions. Exhibiting compassion does not mean allowing others to do what they want when they want. Instead, compassion means knowing when to exhibit gentle encouragement, stern resolve, and the courage to part paths knowing each person has their own journey. Although compassion is needed to help survivors move along their journey of healing, it is not enough to maintain the equilibrium of mental well-being as a steward of trauma.

| Blue | Hope | Blue Lantern Corps | Members of the Blue Lantern Corps represent the embodiment of hope. They believe, beyond the shadow of a doubt, that no matter how bad the circumstances, all will be well. Blue Lantern, Saint Walker deputizes Barry Allen (Flash) to wear the blue ring when battling the Black Lanterns of *Blackest Night*. Similar to Blue Lanterns and Barry Allen, caregivers exhibit this belief that all will be well. Unfortunately, a caregiver's well of hope is not boundless. It must be replenished. This can only be accomplished by taking the needed time to remain centered. This emotion also cannot exist on its own. With it, balance can only be achieved by also having the courage and will of a Green Lantern to anticipate the coming of the approaching dawn. |
| Violet | Love | Star Sapphires | Love is the source of Wonder Woman's power |

				as a superhero, and it is what Star Sapphires use to fuel their violet light. Wonder Woman is deputized as a Star Sapphire after possessing the will, love, and compassion to fend off the effects of a Black Lantern power ring. As a caregiver, love is essential to help survivors heal. Unfortunately, many caregivers are taught that love is an emotion that can only be reserved for survivors. However, caregivers must also have love for themselves if they are going to be good stewards of trauma. Love is a powerful emotion, but without balance it can easily transform into hate and rage. To maintain balance, love is usually accompanied by compassion to allow caregivers the courage, knowledge, and wisdom of when to exhibit love and understanding, but also the compassion to

			allow each the freedom to proceed along their own journey of healing, and the avarice needed to ground their own mental well-being.
Orange	Avarice	Agent Orange	Orange Lanterns are filled with avarice. The need for selfishness, jealously, and possession motivates their actions. While Orange Lanterns are portrayed somewhat as villains throughout *Blackest Night*, more caregivers need to embrace pieces of what distinguishes Agent Orange from other Lanterns. By nature, caregivers are selfless, placing the needs and wants of others before themselves. This may be what makes them good caregivers. However, it also is the primary catalyst for compassion fatigue. Embodying the avarice of an Orange Lantern means having the strength and courage to place the same

			importance of their own mental and physical well-being as you would others. Exhibiting a sense of avarice is the only way to maintain balance socially in the workplace and having the ability to put in the work in order to journey down the path of maintaining trauma stewardship.
Yellow	Fear	Sinestro Corps	Yellow Lanterns are members of the Sinestro Corps, whose source of power originates from fear of those around them. Caregivers who believe they are exhibiting behaviors of a Yellow Lantern are filled with so much fear they are unable to act on their emotions, feeling paralyzed. They are fearful of answering the phone, talking with their peers, or making a mistake that could negatively affect the survivors they are trying to help heal. While fear can be a motivator,

			causing individuals to jump into action too much for too long can result in compassion fatigue.
Red	Rage	Red Lantern Corps	Members of the Red Lantern Corps are filled with so much rage that red plasma shoots from their mouths with the intensity of napalm. Their anger blinds them from reason, causing them to be unable to speak or recognize their actions, preventing them from recognizing friend from foe. Caregivers can experience the same blinding rage of a Red Lantern when experiencing secondary traumatic stress. While anger is useful and necessary to do the work of helping survivors heal, too much can transform into rage for a broken system or inadequate administrators that can become secondary traumatic stress. Anger can be a motivator to do

			the work that others may be unwilling or unable to accomplish. It may have even been the catalyst to push a caregiver to leave the confines of their Paradise Island to help trauma survivors. Visit the emotion. Allow it to motivate your actions, but do not allow it to consume you in the manner it consumes Red Lanterns.
Black	Death	Black Lanterns	In *Blackest Night,* the members of the Black Lantern Corps are those who have been reanimated to life, feeding on the emotions of others because they have none of their own. Caregivers who believe they are exhibiting behaviors of Black Lanterns are numb to their emotions due to feelings of being burned out. In an attempt to limit the negative impact of their emotions, these caregivers dissociate from their emotions.

			While everyone has the potential to dissociate from time to time, too much can cause lasting burnout.

Chapter Thirteen
Achieving Atonement

"We cannot be complete if we are kept from our true purpose."
—**Mera**, *Wonder Woman #750*, "To Me" (2020)

Diana's journey as a hero began with the crash landing of Steve Trevor on Paradise Island. His arrival catapulted her Call to Adventure as Wonder Woman, taking her from the safety and perfection of Themyscira to "man's world" as the Amazon ambassador of peace and justice. Unfortunately, her Road of Trials as hero led to the loss of friends such as Dr. Barbara Ann Minerva, loss of love with the parting of ways from Steve Trevor, and the loss of her identity as Wonder Woman with the breaking of her Bracelets of Submission and the stealing of her crown and lasso by the villain Cheetah. Diana is not able to achieve reconciliation for her past actions until she confronts the mistakes of the past, seeks to find the truth in her actions as Wonder Woman, and begins mending the past to become stronger and wiser in the future when returning to Themyscira and seeking atonement with the help of her mother, Queen Hippolyta.

After defeating Cheetah, Diana was able to regain her sense of love and compassion, allowing her the ability to regain her stolen crown and golden lasso from the villain. However, Diana's Bracelets of Submission were shattered beyond repair. To regain possession of her final weapon, Diana returned to Themyscira in 2002's *Wonder Woman #750*, "The Wild Hunt: Finale" to seek guidance from her mother to reconcile both of their mistakes of the past.

Diana speaks with her mother at an altar atop a mountain on Themyscira meant for reflection of past mistakes. Laid before them are the shards of her mother's shattered Bracelets of Submission. Queen Hippolyta tells her daughter, "These bracelets are mine, shattered by Herakles in the uprising that freed the Amazons. They helped liberate and lead our people. Today, we reforge them. As mother and daughter." Together, Diana and Hippolyta reforge the bracelets to make them into the strongest bracelets worn by any Amazon.

The design of Diana's new Bracelets of Submission are not beautiful in the traditional sense. Instead, the silver of the bracelets is splintered with the orange metal of Amazonium. Although they are not perfect, the bracelets are a healthy blend of both the past and present, making them more powerful because of reconciling the mistakes of the past rather than simply living with them. Diana uses these bracelets to redefine her mission of peace and truth as the ambassador for the Amazons on her own terms rather than those of the gods. Afterward, Hippolyta tells Diana:

> Orna tells me you've refocused your mission on your own terms. As queen, I worry. But as your mother, I could not be prouder. Since we broke our chains, we've been rebels. Since I named you, you've been a hunter. And that hunt, that mission, more than ever is for truth. And the truth is an act of rebellion. The only hunt. The one true mission of Wonder Woman.

Here, Diana has done more than Cross the First Threshold. She has learned from the mistakes of her past to become stronger and wiser in her pursuit of the truth and need to achieve balance throughout her life. This is what it means to achieve Atonement, and it is the next step on a caregiver's journey of healing.

Atonement

Crossing the First Threshold often leads to the reflection of thoughts, feelings, and actions that were made while experiencing burnout, compassion fatigue, or secondary traumatic stress. Reflection does not mean obsessive rumination of past mistakes.

Instead, Atonement is a caregiver realizing that mistakes were made in the past in order to forgive themselves of their perceived or real mistakes, becoming stronger when learning to identify their own shortcomings and leaning on others for support when needed. Acknowledging that mistakes may have been made in the past while seeking to regain balance does not mean being a hypocrite. It is a sign of growth that leads to strength. Ares, the Greek god of war, helps to prove this when facing the truth of his actions when trapped in the Golden Perfect of Wonder Woman.

Atonement of Ares

In 1987's graphic novel, *Wonder Woman: Gods and Mortals* by George Perez, Ares, the Greek god of war, has a single goal he desperately wishes to achieve at any cost—to decimate the status quo of power structures throughout Earth and Mount Olympus, leaving him the single greatest (and only) power throughout the universe. The only way he knows to achieve this goal is through the perpetuation of war, misinformation, and hatred. These means of achieving his goal are well articulated when his son, Deimos, speaks the same words of hatred to the two primary nations of the world with nuclear weapons. In an auditorium of the rich, powerful, and influential in the United States, and later in Russia, he tells them:

> *Welcome, my children, to the House of Deimos! Soon, all you have worked and waited for will at last be yours! For the hour at last is upon us my children! The moment is come for us to strike! For years we have watched helplessly as this great nation has been overrun by imbeciles, by those who do not love this country as we do, by those who seek to subvert all that which we believe! If this nation is to be strong, we must be strong, strong enough to crush those who would defy us! Nothing must be permitted to interfere with our plan to protect our country, to protect our power! Go now, my children, and do what must be done! Make them fear us, for that fear shall give you strength!*

Throughout the graphic novel, with the help of Steve Trevor and Etta Candy, Wonder Woman battles the minions of the ARIES Project from detonating numerous nuclear weapons across the planet. In the final battle between hero and villain, Diana discovers it is impossible to defeat Ares with her fists, sword, or Bracelets of Submission. Instead, she is only able to defeat the god of war by showing him the truth behind the consequences of his actions.

Using the Golden Perfect, Wonder Woman wraps the lasso around the waist of Ares to show him the consequences if he is allowed to carry out his actions. Between graphic depictions of fire, ash, and mayhem, Perez writes:

> And suddenly, Ares can see the awesome mushroom clouds rising shroud life over the Earth's greatest cities. Suddenly, he can feel the heat from the blossoming fireballs stripping flesh from bone, reducing bone to ash, laying waste to all the world! For one brief incandescent moment, as a fiery tide sweeps relentlessly across the land, Ares is truly and finally master of the world, and then he is alone, his kingdom a charred and smoking cinder, devoid of life and thus devoid of purpose. Aye, enveloped by the lasso of truth, Ares sees—truly sees—the ultimate consequences of his actions, and for the first time in his immortal existence, the war-god weeps. For, without those alive to worship him, Ares' power swiftly wanes, his great palace Areopagus growing more and more decayed, until, at last, it crumbles into nothingness, carrying the war-god with it down into the vile dust whence he first sprung, unmourned, unhonored, and unsung.

Afterward, Ares realizes his mistake and seeks to restore balance to the universe. He destroys his war zombies, preventing the launch of nuclear warheads. He does not vanish from existence, but realizes he is one piece of a larger equation. He explains his ability to atone for his past when he tells Diana:

> Tolliver (one of Ares' minions) is gone, as is his Soviet counterpart! The threat is ended! The balance restored! His

capacity for bloodshed is great, and this shall keep me strong, but I shall never again take an active role in man's demise! It seems those days are past! There is a difference between destruction and oblivion, child, and it falls to you to teach it to man, to save man from himself! We shall see if you are equal to it! And if you are not, Diana, then beware! For the world shall hear from me again!

When navigating the paths of trauma stewardship, caregivers must be like Ares when atoning for past mistakes. The god of war did not deny his nature or his past actions. Instead, knowing his actions were wrong, he realized his grandiose belief in himself as the most important and powerful of all the Greek gods and the need to acquire more and more power had become too great. Caregivers who reach Atonement in their journey of healing should come to realize the grandiosity of their actions in the same way. This means understanding that, regardless of who we are, whether a professional caregiver or a loved one of a survivor, each of us is human. This means that regardless of who we are, or the nature of our profession, mistakes will be made. However, rather than pretending as though the mistakes of the past never took place, caregivers must seek to hold themselves and others accountable for their actions. This is the only way to grow and move toward achieving balance.

Healing Through Atonement

Achieving the ability to reflect over past actions as a professional caregiver or loved one of a survivor of childhood trauma takes the courage, will, love, and self-compassion of Crossing the First Threshold. Unfortunately, the buzz word that has begun to commonly be used throughout society is *self-care.* The problem with the term self-care is not only is the definition of the word too broad, but it has become synonymous with meditation and practicing yoga, meaning self-care is not trauma stewardship. This is because while self-care techniques such as yoga and meditation are helpful in achieving balance, the pressure of feeling as though there is a need to juggle yet another task on top of the pressure and stress of helping survivors heal when time restraints may not always make it possible. Believing there is a *need* to practice self-care rather than a *want* to only causes more feelings of burnout, compassion fatigue, and secondary traumatic stress.

Instead, trauma stewardship means achieving balance when taking the time to metabolize, understand, and process feelings of stress and secondary trauma in moments throughout the day. Although these moments are brief, they require practice. One way to achieve this practice is through the use of SOS.

The self-help guide by Julian Ford and Jon Wortman, *Hijacked by Your Brain: How to Free Yourself When Stress Takes Over*, discusses methods for individuals to better manage their feelings of stress rather than attempting to eliminate feeling stress (which Ford and Wortman argue is an impossibility.) Similar to techniques used during cognitive behavior therapy to change negative automatic thoughts created by cognitive distortions, Ford and Wortman provide mental focusing techniques to help individuals remain in control of managing their stress, whether high or low.

One useful method discussed throughout the book is SOS. This technique is used to quickly help individuals understand what may not only be causing them stress, but also lack of control managing that stress. The technique is used to quickly help individuals understand that although they may be highly stressed, they can simultaneously be highly in control of him or herself. This means that high stress and high levels of personal control are not mutually exclusive, but are in fact synergistic. This is similar to Wonder Woman, who may experience the stress of strategizing a winning battle plan in the midst fighting but maintains control by remaining grounded in her abilities and wisdom as an Amazon. While SOS is the universal call of distress, the acronym SOS is similar when helping caregivers reduce their level of distress.

Here are the steps:

- **Step back:** Stepping back is the first step caregivers can take when needing to center themselves and reduce their level of stress. During this step, individuals should strive to be present, pause, slow down, and clear their mind of swirling thoughts to access their emotions and their level of stress.

- **Orient:** The next step is to orient what it is that the individual believes is the most important thing in their life that would be able to reduce the amount of stress. This means making a single, clear (but not easy) choice about what they care about. This form of orientation is larger than the need for money or fame. Instead, it is centered in achieving lasting happiness and safety.

- **Self-check:** The final step in the SOS process is similar to the first. This is because when an individual performs a self-check and takes a rating of their stress level, if after reorienting their thoughts their stress level has not decreased, then the caregiver should begin the process again.

To complete this process, caregivers must be capable of understanding their emotions. The emotion chart in the previous chapter, "Crossing the First Threshold," can help professional caregivers and loved ones of childhood sexual abuse survivors navigate the Atonement of their past to prevent burnout, compassion fatigue, and secondary traumatic stress.

Chapter Fourteen
Becoming the Master of Two Worlds

"She told me that to love and lose and hurt and heal is human."

—**Kara**, *Wonder Woman #750,* "To Me" (2020)

A hero's journey often ends with the hero returning to their place of birth. However, they return to their Paradise Island changed. Their trials, triumphs, and shortcomings have provided them with a wisdom and insight that has been elevated above the wisdom of others. Diana exhibits this elevation of insight in the graphic novel *Kingdom Come* (1996).

In the alternate future of *Kingdom Come*, the anger Diana felt following the loss of her identity as an Amazon eventually manifested itself in the form of rage. Over time, that rage grew into a hatred for the new generation of metahumans and their lack of a moral compass when it came to defending those who cannot protect themselves. Fortunately, by the end of the novel, with the help and guidance of other heroes such as Superman and Batman, Diana realizes the error of her ways and atones for her past, no longer striving to become a warrior, but instead a mentor to a new generation of heroes. The novel explains how: "Through her courage, the princess is at last granted her crown. No longer does she see herself as a failed student. She is a teacher whose work is just beginning."

Her journey leads her not only back to Themyscira, but man's world as well. She becomes the **Master of Two Worlds**, achieving the final goal of not only a hero, but a caregiver's journey of healing as well.

Master of Two Worlds

Following a caregiver's Crossing of the First Threshold and self-reflection of Atonement, they develop the ability to become a Master of Two Worlds. In this final stage, no longer is the Apotheosis of bliss and happiness followed immediately by the Abyss of sadness due to the grandiose beliefs and practices of one's job as a professional caregiver or helpful guidance of a survivor as a friend of loved one. Instead, a healthy balance of professional and social life has been achieved. Professional caregivers and loved ones of survivors are able to balance work, relationships, and their personal activities in a way that is beneficial to helping survivors heal while maintaining their own sense of mental and physical well-being.

These caregivers are also capable of leaning on one another for needed support and helping guide other caregivers who may be experiencing burnout, compassion fatigue, and secondary traumatic stress through their own journey of healing. Using the wisdom they have gained, these caregivers influence others in a way that has the potential to transform the climate and culture of a workplace or home in a manner that reduces the possibility of stress from manifesting.

Let the Fire Burn

What makes Wonder Woman truly powerful, wise, and beautiful is not her ability fight or her perfectly symmetrical face. It's her ability to not only connect with the compassion and love of others, but also attend to the needs of nature. She does not seek to simply find solutions to satisfy the needs of people, but understands that the Earth is a living thing with needs of its own that must be fulfilled if balance is going to be achieved. She demonstrates her ability to navigate her mastery of two worlds, even against the suggestions and wishes of other superheroes.

In the graphic novel *Wonder Woman: Down to Earth* (2004) by Greg Rucka, there is a scene in which Diana demonstrates her understanding of the complexities of compassion and love when she tells Flash to let a forest fire burn itself out and run its course. She tells the fastest man alive, "The forest needs this fire, Flash. It's how it grows; it's how it stays healthy. If you pull the air from it, you will serve nothing but the now to the pain of the future. The next fire will be worse."

Unfortunately, Flash does not understand Diana's logic. Although the homes of local residents are safe from fire damage, he believes the forest fire could result in the loss of all the wildlife if the fire is not stopped. Instead of growing angry, frustrated, or annoyed, she calmly explains to Flash in the midst of raging flames how all the life in the woods will not die. She says, "Death is necessary, Flash. It is part of life, and if we say life is a blessing, we must say that death is a blessing as well. Let the fire burn."

Flash does not agree with her beliefs, but he does not deny its truth. He knows that although he is a chemical scientist, he does not have the same insight and wisdom as Diana because of her roles as Amazon warrior, peace ambassador, princess of Themyscira, and god of war following the death of Ares.

Diana lives and navigates multiple worlds with calm understanding, patience, compassion, love, and courage in the same manner caregivers must become the Master of Two Worlds after traveling through their journey of healing. It is true that other professional caregivers or loved ones of survivors may not understand the thoughts and actions of these trauma stewards in the same way Flash does not understand or agree with Diana's decision to let the fire run its course. However, rather than become grandiose in their beliefs of healing, balance, and trauma stewardship, these caregivers must demonstrate the same compassion, patience, and love as Wonder Woman in an attempt to become mentors to others who may be experiencing burnout, compassion fatigue, and secondary traumatic stress when first beginning their journey of healing. These caregivers learn and help teach other caregivers to lean on one another when the load becomes too difficult to bear.

Becoming the Master of Two Worlds as a caregiver does not mean that life is now easy and you have all the answers. In fact, it means just the opposite. It means acknowledging you are human and that mistakes will be made, but no one should feel they have to journey along the path of healing alone. It means knowing when there is a need to step away from the desk, phone, computer, or patient to recalibrate. It also means knowing when to show the needed compassion for others, not letting a survivor become avoidant, and when to demonstrate the needed compassion for yourself to leave an unchangeable, toxic work environment or victim that is causing severe psychological and/or physical harm. While some may believe demonstrating this form of compassion is a form of weakness or lack of grit, that is not true. Instead, it demonstrates the ability to grow, heal, and become wise.

Each of us have the ability to become overwhelmed—meaning each of us sometimes need help maintaining a sense of balance throughout our professional and social lives. Some may need more help than others, but as a caregiver who has made the conscious decision to leave their Paradise Island, it is your responsibility to not only help survivors heal from the C-PTSD of childhood trauma, but maintain your own sense of mental and physical well-being. This is how we build communities capable and eager to help one another grow, recover, and engage with one another through tough times. This is how we save our inner Wonder Woman.

Growing Strong and Offering Strength to Others

There is no tool that can be applied to this guide that would demonstrate how to become the Master of Two Worlds. It requires the needed ten thousand hours of practice that only comes with time, patience, and fortune. However, I will end this chapter with a great Wonder Woman comic that helps to sum up what it means to help others discover their own sense of inner strength.

As professional caregivers and loved ones of survivors of childhood trauma we offer each survivor something different. For some, it's love. For others, it's compassion. The Wonder Woman comic "To Me" in *Wonder Woman #750* (2020) demonstrates how each caregiver who makes the decision to enter the Belly of the Whale offers survivors the opportunity to mature and grow in a way they did not know was necessary to complete their journey as a hero.

Steve Trevor learned healing is not a weakness. He remembers their relationship over the years and how she was strong and a capable fighter: "But no matter her fury, her power, her strength, I knew her first as a healer. I was ... haunted by the things I had seen. She stayed with me. Held me in my nightmares. She taught me that scars are not shames, and all healing is a journey. She taught me to heal myself. For that, I'll always love her."

Caregivers who enter the Belly of the Whale and make the choice to heal their inner Wonder Woman not only heal survivors of trauma, but help provide them with the courage to make the decision to heal themselves. Survivors of C-PTSD can believe that healing is a sign of weakness. Modeling the journey of healing and leading by example helps survivors and their caregivers defeat the shame associated with seeking help.

Mera learned that love is not a sign of weakness. Similar to child survivors of childhood sexual abuse, Mera's past taught her that trusting and loving others was too dangerous of a risk. However, Diana taught her that not all relationships are toxic. Mera explains this when she narrates:

> But coming up from the darkness of the past ... from the
> depth of pain from the family and birthright that cast me out.
> What a little thing it is to love another and feel held by them in

return. What a little thing, to hold the entire world . . . I learned to love because of her, and it's true what they say—it really is the only thing that can save the world.

Caregivers who cross the first threshold and learn to navigate all of their emotions help provide survivors with the courage to feel all of their emotions as well. Learning to love is not a weakness, and caregivers who heal their inner Wonder Woman help spread this wisdom throughout the world.

Kara learned the strength of leaning on others in times of weakness. Following the loss of Stargirl, Kara lost the will to fly. Rather than provide words of wisdom about a loss she has not experienced herself, Diana offers the strength of her friendship and truths she does know are true. She tells Kara:

Grief means she was real. Grief means that she mattered. As you matter. As this matters. As it always will. It will hurt today, and tomorrow, and a year from now, and ten years from now. It may even hurt forever. But it will not always hurt the same. What do we do with grief? We do the best we can. And I will be your friend for as long as you will have me. And I will be here for you as you discover all that awaits.

Rather than being told that the pain eventually fades, or that moving on is the best way to get over grief, Diana expressed her wisdom of knowing that each individual's journey is their own. No matter how hard a caregiver may wish to heal those they love and care for, each individual must heal on their own terms and in their own time. All a caregiver can do is provide survivors with the knowledge that the ability to recover and heal is possible with time. Healing your inner Wonder Woman means providing support to others when they need it the most, and to accept that support when it is needed.

Each individual explains the true strength of Wonder Woman when they state, "What she taught us was not love, or strength, or how to grieve, or how to heal. She taught us our own magnificent power." Caregivers who choose to leave the safety of their Paradise Island do not do so knowing they have to help others. They do so because they want to. They do so because they discover their own strength in helping others. Diana explains this on the final page of the comic when she says:

> They say I have been so many things to them. I never meant to be. But I am grateful all the same. What a life I might have had a princess of Themyscira . . . and yet, no matter the world, and no matter the time, I think I would always choose, and choose, and choose again. I would always leave paradise and go into the world of mortals, suffering, and pain. What purpose is there but this? To try to do good, be good, do and be better, and kinder, and wiser than before. I have seen all I have been to others. What am I to myself? I do this because I am this. I hope that is enough.

Save your inner Wonder Woman to continue to provide the same strength, love, courage, and compassion to others in the same way you show them to yourself when you have learned to become the Master of Two Worlds.

Chapter Fifteen
Choosing to Become the Master of Two Worlds (Autobiographical)

"I do not fear my own strength. And I am more than what love made me. Even when love fades, justice remains, and I will pursue it with the last breath in my body."

—**"Wonder Woman"**, *Wonder Woman #79*, "Loveless: Part 3" (2019)

Whether we believe or not, we are not superheroes. The impact of the consistent gravity of the world eventually becomes too much to bear and the release valve must be engaged. If not, the pressure of life becomes too great, causing each of us to either implode inward on ourselves or explode outward with rage. Unfortunately, survivors of childhood sexual abuse can tell when the pressures of life become too much for their caregivers to handle. This is why, if for no other reason, you as a caregiver make the decision to save your inner Wonder Woman and become the Master of Two Worlds. Do it for those you are seeking to help heal.

Survivors of childhood sexual abuse deserve to have caregivers who operate at peak performance and are willing to help them comfort the trauma of their past abuse. If these caregivers are not capable of the task, the survivors are able to tell. I learned this lesson as a secondary English teacher after returning to my desk at the end of a lesson and discovering a folded, handwritten letter addressed to "Mr. Rogers" resting on the keyboard of my laptop.

It had been decades since I had received a middle school note. Before that moment, I didn't know kids still wrote notes by hand. I believed it was all Snapchats and TikToks. Seeing the note sitting on my computer, my brain immediately returned to the letters marked "For Your Eyes Only" that I received between the ringing of class bells at Sterling Middle School—the letters I still have, and sometimes read, from long forgotten friends and those I wished would have become more.

However, this letter on my laptop was different. It did not radiate the same aura of happiness, excitement, cheer, and potential for possibilities as I held it in my hand. Instead, it was something ominous. Something to be feared. This is because, as a teacher, there is the need to wear different hats as a trauma counselor, and letters such as these usually do not result in positivity when addressed specifically to a teacher. As a twenty-first-century educator, I knew that its contents were most likely something I would have to report to either the administration, a school counselor, or child protective services. While unfolding the edges of the page and smoothing the creases, there were no longer feelings of reminiscent butterflies from days long past. Instead, racing thoughts were filled with dread and fear about what I would learn about one of my students.

The letter (luckily) did not contain any information in need of being reported to the administration, but its contents were troubling. To my surprise, it did not involve the coming-of-age problems of one of my students. But to my sadness, it involved my inability to create a positive learning environment for all my students due to my own recognizable feelings of burnout and compassion fatigue. This student wrote me a letter to let me know that she noticed I was not as happy and cheerful as I normally was in the classroom. She wrote:

> *Hey, you doing ok? You seem kind of upset lately. I just want you to know that I'm always here to talk, even though I'm just a kid. I have been through a lot. I don't know your full life story, but I will understand. Every time I walk into your class, I get this feeling of joy. It's like a safe place for me. I know you probably don't want to talk to a kid about what's going on in your life, but*

I don't want you to think about hurting yourself or something. I hate seeing you upset. It breaks my heart. I know you're older than me and you have had more experiences, but life is hard, I know. Sometimes I just don't want to be alive, but we have to push through because if you don't who will be there when I graduate? Who's going to be there when I get my first job, my first paycheck. Who's going to be there when your kids have their first kiss or when they start high school. The whole school loves you. We all love your stupid jokes and when you tell us stories. I would hate to find out that one day my favorite teacher isn't here anymore. Thinking about you gone is hard enough. Even if you don't want to talk to me, you can talk to another teacher or a friend. Talk to someone if you decide not to talk to me. If it's about your son, I know it hurts. I lost my uncle, and he was like a dad to me. He was the dad I will never have.

The thing about those who have suffered C-PTSD is that they are intuitive to the emotions and behaviors of those around them. This is especially true when the individual's survival and safety depends on a person of power. What this student recognized when writing this letter is that I was experiencing pain and sadness that I believed could easily be hidden from my students. While my emotions may have been able to be hidden from most of my students, those who had experienced C-PTSD could read me like a book. The energy I exhibited in class and throughout the school let me know whether or not it was safe for my students to be themselves around me, to feel safe.

This letter helped to demonstrate that if I did not take care of my mental well-being, I was making my classroom feel like an unsafe learning environment. They no longer felt safe enough to be themselves and so could not feel comfortable enough to learn. This did not mean that I needed to fake it better. It meant that I needed to take better care of myself by practicing better trauma stewardship. This did not mean working harder at designing my lessons, but doing better at being human by leaving my classroom to have lunch with my coworkers, leaving work on time a few days a week to workout, smile in the hallway, talk to my coworkers and my wife about the ins and outs of the day. Not to cynically complain about the shortcomings of my students, but to tell stories about the students I love that are both funny, infuriating, and everything in-between. It was the only way I not only ensured having a fun and safe learning environment, but I felt pleasant enough to be a good father to my daughters and husband to my wife. This letter helped me realize the necessity of maintaining balance, practicing trauma stewardship, and becoming a master of two worlds. It not only made me a better trauma informed educator, but a well-balanced human being.

Further Reading

"Still, the funny thing was, for all her abilities, it wasn't what she could do that changed things. No, it was what she saw each of us capable of doing that changed us, changed everything. She was the first superhero. And yet it was the heroism she saw in each of us that shined a new way forward. A way out of the dark."

—President Franklin D. Roosevelt, *Wonder Woman #750*, "A Brave New World" (2020)

Wonder Woman is an amazing superhero! Her ability to show compassion and love while also possessing the ability to decimate her opponents into submission is one of the many reasons she has remained a beloved hero for eight decades. I did not truly begin to understand the depth of her appeal until recently. It is for this reason I highly recommend reading the Wonder Woman comics explained throughout this guide. Although Wonder Woman comics are referenced throughout *How to Save Your Inner Wonder Woman* to assist in understanding the effects and how to heal from burnout, compassion fatigue, and secondary traumatic stress, the descriptions provided throughout the guide do not do them the proper justice. The ability to blend graphics with words is what makes comics unique in their ability to tell a story. It is for this reason I strongly encourage each reader of this guide to take the time to read a few (if not all) of these amazing tales listed below. Other helpful books, guides, and workbooks are listed as well for those seeking to further their knowledge of trauma stewardship.

All-Star Comics #8, "Introducing Wonder Woman." (1941)

Blackest Night: Wonder Woman, "Part 1: The Living" (2009)

Blackest Night: Wonder Woman, "Part 2: Black Lantern Wonder Woman" (2009)

Blackest Night: Wonder Woman, "Part 3: A Hint of Daylight" (2009)

Flashpoint (2011)

Heroes, Villains, and Healing: A Guide for Male Survivors of Childhood Sexual Abuse Using DC Comic Superheroes and Villains by Kenneth Rogers Jr.

Hijacked by Your Brain: How to Free Yourself When Stress Takes Over by Julian Ford and Jon Wortman

How to Kill Your Batman: A Guide for Male Survivors of Childhood Sexual Abuse Using Batman to Heal Hypervigilance by Kenneth Rogers Jr.

How to Master Your Inner Superman: A Guide for Male Survivors of Childhood Sexual Abuse Using Superman to Conquer the Need for Facades by Kenneth Rogers Jr.

Infinite Crisis (2006)

Justice (2007)

Justice League #7, "The Totality: Conclusion" (2018)

Justice League #32, "Justice / Doom War, Part 3" (2019)

Justice League #36, "Justice / Doom War: Part 7" (2020)

Justice League #42, "Justice Lost: Part 4" (2018)

Justice League #44, "Cold War Part One: Monster Within" (2020)

Justice League #49, "The Darseid War: Part 9" (2016)

Kingdom Come (1996)

Overcoming Compassion Fatigue: A Practical Resilience Workbook (2014) by Martha Teater and John Ludgate

Raped Black Male: A Memoir by Kenneth Rogers Jr.

Reducing Compassion Fatigue, Secondary Traumatic Stress and Burnout: A Trauma-Sensitive Workbook by William Steele

Real Boys: Rescuing Our Sons from the Myths of Boyhood by William S. Pollack

Sensation Comics Featuring Wonder Woman #1 "Gothamazon" (2014)

Superman: Red Son (2014)

Superman/Wonder Woman Volume 4: Dark Truth (2016)

Superman/Wonder Woman Volume 5 "A Savage End" (2017)

The Body Keeps the Score by Bessel Van der Kolk

The Complex PTSD Workbook by Arielle Schwartz

The Courage to Heal by Ellen Bass and Laura Davis

The Hero with A Thousand Faces by Joseph Campbell

Trauma and Recovery by Judith Herman

Trauma Stewardship by Laura van Dernoot Lipsky

Wonder Woman #1, "The Lies" (2016)

Wonder Woman #8, "Interlude" (2016)

Wonder Woman # 16, "God Watch: Part One" (2017)

Wonder Woman #18, "God Watch: Part Two" (2017)

Wonder Woman #24, "Godwatch: Epilogue" (2017)

Wonder Woman #28, "Heart of the Amazon" (2016)

Wonder Woman #38, "Swan's Song: Part 1" (2018)

Wonder Woman #39, "Swan's Song: Part 2" (2018)

Wonder Woman #40, "Swan's Song: Conclusion" (2018)

Wonder Woman #51, "The Fifty-Second Visit" (2018)

Wonder Woman #58, "The Just War: Part 1" (2018)

Wonder Woman #64, "The Grudge" (2019)

Wonder Woman #76, "Mothers and Children" (2019)

Wonder Woman #77, "Loveless: Part 2" (2019)

Wonder Woman #78, "Loveless: Part 2" (2019)

Wonder Woman #79, "Love's End" (2019)

Wonder Woman #80, "Loveless: Part 4" (2019)

Wonder Woman #82, "The Wild Hunt: Part 1" (2019)

Wonder Woman #99, "Top Secret" (1958)

Wonder Woman #107, "Wonder Woman Amazon Teen-Ager" (1968)

Wonder Woman #177, "Paradise Found" (2002)

Wonder Woman # 195, "The Mission" (2003)

Wonder Woman #288, "Swan Song" (1982)

Wonder Woman #750, "To Leave Paradise" (2020) "Always" "To Me" "The Wild Hunt: Finale"

Wonder Woman #754, "The Truth Usurps" (2020)

Wonder Woman #755, "The Four Horsewomen: Part 1" (2020)

Wonder Woman: Down to Earth (2004)

Wonder Woman: Earth One Volume Two (2018)

Wonder Woman: Gods and Mortals (1987)

Wonder Woman Volume #1, "Blood" (2013)

Wonder Woman Volume 2 #219, "Sacrifice, Part IV" (2005)

Wonder Woman: Volume #2, "Guts," (2012)

Wonder Woman Volume #7, "War-Torn" (2016)

GLOSSARY

Examine yourself, Hippolyte. Examine your race. Once, the Amazons dreamed of leading mankind! But you chose to withdraw from humanity, to ignore the purpose for which you were created, and you grew bitter and corrupt. Have you forgotten the source of your power? Have you forgotten the example you were to set?"

—**Athena**, *Wonder Woman #1* "The Princess and the Power" (1987)

The world of comic books can be confusing at times. This is especially true for *Wonder Woman*. The reason for this is that reading a Wonder Woman comic book often requires being capable of navigating Greek mythology. Learning to navigate these different worlds and understand their connections to one another was one of the primary difficulties when beginning to research and write this guide. This glossary is meant to help readers understand some of the many characters, their abilities, locations, and weapons used throughout the Wonder Woman comics.

A

Agent Orange: The group of power lanterns from the DC comic event *Blackest Night*, fueled by avarice and representing the color orange on the emotional spectrum. The most popular Orange Lantern is Larfleeze, who has the ability to create mental constructs with his power ring.

Amazon Warriors: A group of female warriors blessed with long life who originated from the souls of women who had been killed prematurely by the men they trusted. After overthrowing their capture by Herakles, they shielded themselves from the outside world on invisible Paradise Island.

Aphrodite: The Greek goddess of love and one of the patrons of the Amazon warriors.

Ares: The Greek god of war.

ARGUS: A secret United States government facility that operates under the Department of Homeland Security and is commanded by Colonel Steve Trevor and Amanda Waller. It is an acronym that stands for Advanced Research Group Uniting Super-Humans.

Athena: The Greek goddess of wisdom and one of the patrons of the Amazon warriors.

B

Barbara Ann Minerva: One of Wonder Woman's oldest friends who becomes one of her most dangerous enemies when she is transformed into the villain Cheetah by ancient god, Urzkartaga. Her knowledge of ancient cultures and languages made her a valuable ally to Wonder Woman and her mission of peace.

Batman: One the most powerful superheroes of the DC universe who is also a member of the Justice League. Unlike other superheroes, he has no metahuman abilities.

Black Lanterns: The group of power lanterns from the DC comic event *Blackest Night* that have the ability to raise the dead with the use of black power rings. Once a black power ring has acquired a host, the connection can only be severed when multiple power rings on the emotional spectrum merge to create a white light.

Blue Lantern Corps: The group of power lanterns from the DC comic event *Blackest Night* that are fueled with hope and represents the color blue on the emotional spectrum. Their primary power is the ability to create mental constructs with the use of their power rings. The most popular of the Blue Lanterns is Saint Walker.

Bracelets of Submission: One of Wonder Woman's most powerful and memorable weapons that is worn on her wrist and possesses the power to deflect bullets and provide protection from other attacks.

C

Cheetah: One of Wonder Woman's most deadly enemies who used to be one of her closest friends after being transformed into a villain by ancient god, Urzkartaga. Her deadliness not only comes from the sharpness of her claws, speed, or strength of a cheetah, but also her knowledge of ancient civilizations as Barbara Ann Minerva.

D

Deimos and Phobos: Sons of Ares, the god of war. Deimos is the god of terror, and Phobos is the god of fear.

Diana Prince: The name Diana acquired when leaving Themyscira and the alter ego of Wonder Woman. Unlike the alter ego of other superheroes, Diana and Wonder Woman are very much the same person.

E

Eirene: The Greek goddess of peace.

Etta Candy: One of Wonder Woman's oldest and most trusted friends.

F

Flash: Known as the fastest man alive, Flash's metahuman ability is super speed. As a member of the Justice League, his alter ego is often forensic scientist, Barry Allen.

G

Golden Perfect: One of Wonder Woman's most powerful weapons, the golden lasso was forged by the Greek god Hephaestus, and has the ability to compel an individual who touches it to tell the truth.

Green Lantern Corps: The most popular and well known of the lanterns in the DC universe, they use will and courage to fuel their power rings and represent green on the emotional spectrum. The most popular of the Green Lanterns are Hal Jordan, John Stewart, Kyle Rayner, and Guy Garner.

H

Hephaestus: The Greek god of smithing and fire who forges the weapons of the gods of Olympus.

Hera: The Greek goddess of marriage and women who is also a patron of the Amazon warriors.

Herakles: Also known as Hercules, this demigod was coaxed into enslaving the Amazon warriors by the Greek god of war, Ares.

Hermes: Messenger of the gods of Olympus and patron of thieves.

I

Indigo Tribe: The group of power lanterns from the DC event *Blackest Night* that are fueled by compassion and represent the color indigo on the emotional spectrum.

K

Kara-El: Also known as Supergirl, she is the cousin of Superman and one of the last surviving members of Krypton.

M

Mayfly: A villain who posseses the metahuman ability of super speed and super strength. Her real name is Moon Robinson, and she suffers from hemophilia. After repeated visits from Wonder Woman while in prison, she becomes an ally and friend of the superhero.

Maxwell Lord: A supervillain who possesses the ability to control the thoughts of others causing a trickle of blood to run from his nose. The destruction caused by his mind control of Superman causes Wonder Woman to break his neck while wrapped in the Golden Perfect.

Mera: The queen of Atlantis and close friend of Wonder Woman who possesses the metahuman ability of controlling water.

Mount Olympus: The home of the Greek gods.

P

Paradise Island: The veiled island of the Amazon warriors.

Philippus: Most trusted advisor and highest ranking general for Queen Hippolyta of the Amazons.

Q

Queen Hippolyta: The queen of the Amazons and mother of Diana Prince.

R

Red Lantern Corps: The group of power lanterns from the DC event *Blackest Night* fueled by rage and representing the color red on the emotional spectrum. One of their most notable powers is the ability to spit plasma with the intensity of napalm on their enemies.

S

Silver Swan: A villain possessing the power of flight through the use of metallic wings, a high-pitched scream, and super strength. Also known as Vanessa Kapatelis, her abilities originated after losing the ability to use her legs and being injected with nanobots to help heal her injuries.

Sinestro Corps: The group of power lanterns fueled by fear and representing yellow on the emotional spectrum. Similar to Green Lanterns, Yellow Lanterns have the ability to create mental constructs using their power rings. The most notable Yellow Lantern, and founder of the group, is the former Green Lantern, Sinestro.

Star Sapphires: The group of power lanterns fueled by love and representing violet on the emotional spectrum. Similar to Green

Lanterns, Star Sapphires have the ability to create mental constructs using their power rings. The most notable Star Sapphire is Carol Ferris.

Steve Trevor: Former captain of the Army and leader of ARGUS who crash-landed on Paradise Island, beginning Diana's journey as the superhero Wonder Woman. While he is inconsistent as a love interest, Trevor is one of Wonder Woman's oldest friends and closest ally.

Superman: One of the most powerful and well-known heroes of the DC universe. While possessing numerous abilities such as flight, super speed, super strength, and x-ray vision, he is occasionally portrayed as a love interest of Wonder Woman.

T

Themyscira: The home of the Amazon warriors located on Paradise Island.

U

Urzkartaga: Ancient god who transforms Barbara Ann Minerva into the villain Cheetah.

V

Vanessa Kapatelis: The friend of Wonder Woman who lost the use of her legs. Following the injection of nanobots, the death of her mother, and feelings of neglect from Wonder Woman, she transforms into the villain, Silver Swan.

W

White Lanterns: The group of power lanterns from the DC comic event *Blackest Night* who embody life itself and possess the ability to destroy Black Lanterns by severing their connection to their undead hosts.

Wonder Woman: The Amazonian champion and ambassador of peace who was sent from Paradise Island into "man's world" to fight evil and spread the Amazonian beliefs of love and compassion.

Z

Zeus: The Greek god of lightning.

We'd like to know if you enjoyed the book. Please consider leaving a review on the platform from which you purchased the book

CPSIA information can be obtained
at www.ICGtesting.com
Printed in the USA
LVHW110741161020
668887LV00005B/263